INTIMATE PARTNERS
HIDDEN PATTERNS
IN LOVE RELATIONSHIPS

Books by Clifford J. Sager

Marriage Contracts and Couple Therapy

Books coauthored by Clifford J. Sager

Black Ghetto Family in Therapy
Progress in Group and Family Therapy

Books by Bernice Hunt

Marriage

Books coauthored by Bernice Hunt

Prime Time: A Guide to the Pleasures and
    Opportunities of the New Middle Age
The Divorce Experience

INTIMATE PARTNERS

HIDDEN PATTERNS IN LOVE RELATIONSHIPS

**Clifford J. Sager, M.D.
and Bernice Hunt**

MCGRAW-HILL BOOK COMPANY

New York St. Louis San Francisco Auckland Bogotá
Guatemala Hamburg Johannesburg Lisbon London Madrid
Mexico Montreal New Delhi Panama Paris San Juan
São Paulo Singapore Sydney Tokyo Toronto

First paperback edition, 1981

2 3 4 5 6 7 8 9 0 FG FG 8 7 6 5 4

LIBRARY OF CONGRESS CATALOGING IN PUBLICATION DATA
Sager, Clifford J.   1916–
Intimate partners.
1. Unmarried couples.   2. Interpersonal relations.
3. Intimacy (Psychology)   4. Marriage.
I. Hunt, Bernice Kohn, joint author.   II. Title.
HQ734.S16   301.41   78-26727
ISBN 0-07-054427-1
0-07-054428-X (paperback)

to Anne and Morton

Contents

CHAPTER

1. The Trouble with Couples   1
2. Behavioral Profiles   11
3. Easy—and Uneasy—Alliances   27
4. The Private Covenant   49
5. Rules of the Game   69
6. The Andersons: Their Covenants
   and the Rules of Their Game   83
7. The Sexual Covenant   107
8. The Couple Covenant   129
9. When Negotiations Break Down   153
10. Living Up to the Covenant   173

APPENDIX

A Guide to Writing Your Private
Covenant   189

1

The Trouble with Couples

Bill Williams, junior partner of a law firm, is taking advantage of a quiet Saturday morning to put the finishing touches on a brief. It's an important case, one that could strengthen his chances of becoming a senior partner.

His wife Lucille has gone off to pick up the children; now he hears her car in the driveway. With some irritation he thinks, *She knows I have this work to finish; why couldn't she have kept them out for a couple of hours, taken them to lunch at a drive-in, or something?*

But he puts down his pen and flashes a welcoming smile when Lucille rushes into his study carrying a parcel.

"There's a sale at Gordon's," she tells him. "I stopped on my way to get the kids and picked up this marvelous dress for half price. It's exactly what I need for next Friday." She tears open the box, shakes out the dress, and now holds it up to her shoulders.

"There. Isn't it great?"

"Yes, it's lovely," he says, but it is clear that his feelings do not match the words. His voice expresses irritation rather than appreciation; with a practiced glance, Lucille notes his clenched jaw.

"Listen," she says, her voice suddenly taking on a shrill edge, "I picked out this dress for *your* annual dinner at your boss's next Friday. It's your kind of dress and God knows the price is right. So what's your trouble?"

In all truth, Bill didn't *know* what his trouble was. Everything Lucille said made sense—he liked the dress, and the price *was* right— but he *did* feel annoyed by the purchase.

And so he snapped, "What's *my* trouble? What do you mean *my* trouble? I didn't start this, you did. I *said* the dress is lovely. Isn't that enough? What do you want me to do? Fall on my knees and worship it?"

And once again, the Williams were embroiled in a fight that seemed to rise up from nowhere, a fight that would spoil the weekend, one of a series of fights that were spoiling their lives.

The snow had begun to fall at three o'clock; now, at seven, there was a thick carpet of white over the rooftops, and the street below the apartment house was a sea of wet slush. The late rush-hour traffic had started to subside and Sandra was beginning to feel a knot in her stomach. Where could Ron be? He was an hour late getting home, and he hadn't called. New York traffic was hopeless during snowstorms; Ron might have gotten stalled in a bus; or perhaps he took a cab and it skidded, had an accident. . . .

Sandra had just finished making herself a drink to calm her nerves when she heard Ron's key in the lock.

"Hi, San, I'm here. Boy, whatta trip! I could have been in Philadelphia in the time it took me to go twenty blocks. Hey, say something! Aren't you glad to see me after my Arctic trek? Sore because I didn't lug home a grizzly or a seal or something?"

"Never mind the jokes. Why didn't you call to tell me you'd be late? I don't ask much of you, you know—all I ask is that you call so I don't worry."

"I'm sorry, San, I was only a few minutes late when I left the shop, and I thought if I hurried I might catch a cab and be home on time. I lost a lot of time waiting for one and then finally decided to walk. I passed two phones on the way; one had a waiting line and the other was broken."

"Great, just great! I know damn well that if you got hung up on the way *to* the shop you'd find some way to let precious little Alice know, even if you had to *invent* the telephone!"

"Oh, God. We're not back to that? What's Alice have to do with this? With anything? Why do you have to harp on her?"

"Why do you have to harp on her?" Sandra mimicked. Then, "Why do you insist on having her around? That's the real question. You've admitted yourself that you could probably get your boss to transfer her to another department. You are supposed to be a foreman, aren't you? Doesn't that count for anything? Or is it that you can't get along without her looking at you with those big calf eyes— the two of you mooning over the terrific times you used to have in the sack together?"

"Sandra," Ron pleaded, "Sweetie, I've explained to you a thousand times, I only dated her three times. I never *saw* her again, except at work, after the night I met you. And she doesn't moon over me. She's living with a guy, and she'll probably marry him. You know I can't ask to have her transferred. What am I supposed to say to the boss? My wife says I'm not allowed to work with Alice? This whole conversation's crazy. Don't you know that I love you? And only you? That I don't give a damn about anybody else?"

Sandra's eyes filled with tears; she put her arms around Ron's neck and snuggled close. "I do know, I really do. Oh, why am I such a dope?"

Late that evening, in another house in another city, Ken Lindsay and Linda Gorman were in bed. They had been living together for more than two years and planned to marry the next year, when they finished graduate school and got back East. They both hailed from New England, were amazed and delighted to discover how alike their backgrounds were when they first met in California. As time went on, they seemed to have more and more in common. In a campus society addicted to rock music, Ken and Linda loved baroque; while their peers argued that marriage was passé, Ken and Linda believed that nothing was as important as marriage—and children; each of them, as if confessing a horrible vice, admitted to being clean, neat, and orderly.

The two years of living together had borne out their mutuality, their similar values and goals. Ken and Linda almost never fought. They sometimes had differences of opinion, but when they did, they could always talk about them until they reached some sort of agreement; each was eager to be reasonable, to avoid hurting the other, and above all to return to being in tune with each other.

At first, the couple got along as well in bed as they did anyplace else. Perfectly, they both agreed. But then something strange began to happen. Initially they weren't sure, didn't talk about it. Now it could no longer be ignored.

Linda sat propped against the pillows, running through her notes for tomorrow's exam. Ken lay beside her, waiting for her to turn out the light.

The last time we made love was the night of Joan's party, he mused, *and Linda wasn't turned on. That's a lie. She was worse than not turned on, she was trying to do me a favor, and she hated it. She's seemed bored and distracted during sex for a long time now, but last time, I got the feeling she could hardly wait for it to be over.*

"Honey?" he whispered as the lamp finally went out.

Linda reached over and took his hand. They lay there like that for a few minutes, then Ken began to stroke her shoulder. Almost imperceptibly, Linda inched away.

"Ken," she said, "I'm sorry, but you know I have an early exam in the morning and I *have* to get to sleep."

"Sure, hon, I know. Sleep tight." He kissed her on the cheek and rolled over.

Sonofabitch, he thought, *I'm relieved. I didn't even really want to do it. Two weeks! What the hell's the matter with me?*

Do any of these minidramas with their inconsistent interactions sound familiar? Do they remind you of anyone you know? Of any incidents in your own life? If you are married or involved in a close relationship, your answer is probably *yes,* because, even if you don't draw any absolute parallels, there is one experience almost all couples have in common: At times, they find their behavior—or their problems—impossible to explain. And even if you and your mate have no serious problems, even if you are usually loving and harmonious, there are surely times when one or both of you behave in ways you can't quite grasp.

Partners in badly troubled relationships are often motivated to find out what is going on between them, just as physically sick people are motivated to go to a doctor if they are in enough discomfort. But partners in *good* relationships, or ones that are good enough, are generally willing to drift along as they are, perhaps for a lifetime— or until they separate. Yet, every time some seemingly mysterious mishap takes place, some crossfire that's quite different from what either wanted, they are robbing themselves of the chance for intimacy and mutual satisfaction. They are moving apart instead of together.

It is the aim of this book to throw light on why marital and love relationships prosper or run into difficulties. We suggest that you look at the subject in terms of yourself and the person you love, or may come to love. We will also suggest specific ways you can use the book together, but the extent to which you do so is up to both of you. It could well prove effective as an agent of change, improved understanding, and increased intimacy. Or, it could force you to confront some of the negative aspects of your reactions to each other. If you should find the challenge too difficult or (only rarely does this occur) too upsetting, you might want to seek professional help.

That many of today's couples need to change something is clear. With all the current talk about communication, sharing, equality of the sexes, freedom to grow, and with so many unprecedented opportunities for fulfillment in marriage and quasi-marriage, people presumably should be more content than ever before. But something still isn't working here. We hardly need be reminded of the well-publicized divorce statistics. There has been one divorce for every two marriages, and more than one in three of today's marriages is slated for divorce. It isn't because people don't want to be married:

four out of five (and among the young, virtually all) divorced people marry a second time. So what is wrong?

According to most of the experts, the main problem is that people want marriages that fill their needs, but our needs have changed so radically—and so fast—that many of us don't even know what many of our needs are. And when we do know, we're still in trouble unless our mates know, too; without knowing our needs, how can they possibly fulfill them, even decide whether they want to try to do so or not?

The problem is a modern one, because in the past everyone knew more exactly what marriage was supposed to provide and what each role in it was. Essentially, the man labored on the farm or at a job to provide a home and food. The woman bore the children, took care of them and the house, prepared and served meals from scratch, did the laundry and sewing, nursed the sick and the old, and so forth. A woman was unable to survive without a man to provide for her, and if she didn't marry, she generally lived with her family, as a drudge and baby-sitter. A man couldn't survive without a wife, either. He needed her to raise his brood, to keep him fed, clothed, and comfortable. If a wife died (as they often did) her husband lost no time in finding another. He needed marriage; when survival is the issue, no one worries much about romance and other frills. Some marriages were quite happy, of course, but for many, romantic notions were the stuff of dreams and poetry.

Today, it is becoming the norm for women to work outside the home; they can make it alone—and so can men. We have department stores, supermarkets, restaurants, child-care centers, hospitals, nursing homes, laundromats, and the like to take over many of the former functions of family living. Even friendship and sex are available outside marriage or a similar close relationship. But there are still two needs that cannot be met in any casual connection: love and commitment. Basically, these two elements are exclusive to intimacy; they are the essential benefits we expect to gain from joining forces and if the couple relationship fails to provide them, the partnership is a failure.

It is this shift in our expectation of marriage, the new priority of fulfilling emotional needs rather than external ones, that is creating chaos. The cultural change is still so recent that contemporary couples have no history from which to learn, no models, no guidelines. Life was simpler when everyone knew who cut the firewood, who baked the bread. What is a man's job today, or a woman's? What should a man or a woman do or not do, feel, expect? Few would argue with a woman who enjoys chopping wood or a man who likes to bake bread. They're expressing their own likes, unhampered by old-fashioned roles or stereotypes, happy in their freedom to do so. But if those two—or any two—get together, suddenly the absence of standards confers not just freedom but also confusion. Not simply because they might both chop wood, or both bake bread. Wood and bread are unimportant: if people feel cold they can turn up a thermostat; if they need bread, they can buy it. Such things do not spell survival any more; our most basic needs now are for love and commitment, and the catch is that there are no rules we can follow to make these rewards ours automatically. Even if there were rules, they wouldn't work for everyone, because while physical needs are universal, each couple's emotional needs are, to a large extent, unique. *The challenge, then, for the contemporary couple, is to develop means for emotional survival, ways to get what they now need.*

To meet this challenge, each couple must forge its own precepts. And the only way they can do that is through an understanding of what each one expects, and why they behave as they do. Couples need ongoing dialogues that keep them in touch with each other's feelings and expectations. These must be clearly communicated—and heard. They involve risks—such as fear of exposure, of the other's anger or contempt—but the consequences are usually positive and, at worst, far less damaging than trying to ignore the vague stirrings of unmet wants. Two people with a closeness based on comprehension of themselves and each other form a unit; together, they can maintain themselves—not as their ancestors did, against hostile neighboring tribes, animals, and the elements but against today's enemies: misunderstanding, alienation, and loneliness.

It is no wonder that so many marriages break up, that so many couples who live together decide to separate. "It didn't work out," they say, or "We drifted apart." But why? There are many reasons: an underlying one is that society has moved too fast for most of us. The fact that women have entered industry and the professions and enjoyed working and earning money, the women's movement itself, the sexual revolution, the growth of mass media, computerization, disillusionment with the Establishment, all have combined to change the world too fast for most of us to have absorbed the changes— leaving us in something of a muddle. And couples are in the worst muddle of all.

A contemporary couple may be a married man and woman, a man and a woman who live together, or two people of the same sex who have gotten together. Couples don't have to be married any more; choices are freer; but most people who become couples decide to join together because they are in love.

We generally first feel the need to pair off (or *bond,* in more technical language) in late adolescence. This involves heightened feelings of love, sexual desire, and a wish to be with the other person much of the time, often to the exclusion of others. Often, too, it includes plans to live together, to act as a unit, to bear and raise children; it means sharing hopes and expectations as well as the details of daily life. The initial intensity of being in love usually lasts from a month to three or so years. It is a beautiful and exciting experience that transforms one's emotions and actions; thoughts about the person you love overwhelm you. Many people believe that when these first intense feelings are over the relationship has died. They do not know—or care—how to make the transition from first love to long-term loving. Some experience being in love as exhilaration—without it they find life dull and so they go on to a string of affairs that produce exhilaration for awhile. Each time it is over they are depressed —unless they learn to move on to the additional fulfillment of longer-term loving.

At its best, long-term loving is characterized by a deep acceptance of the other person and oneself, and of the real limitations of each. Both partners assume that they will stay together through all the various phases of life. They are loyal, devoted, have a strong sense of sharing. Their children often strengthen their bond even more. Some partners sustain the intense sexuality of being in love for decades, others settle into a less passionate but no less rewarding relationship. They may encounter conflict, but generally can resolve or live with their differences.

Although many long-term commitments yield joy, others are ugly. We all know unhappy couples with long histories, held together by something. It may be the fear of loneliness, or hostility, or anger; sometimes it is inertia, a fear of developing new relationships, or financial insecurity.

But these are not the relationships we seek. What concerns us in this book is making the transition from short-term to long-term love to produce a partnership of the joyous kind, one in which love remains vital. The transition is not always easy. Couples usually marry during the short-term stage and when they begin to hit snags later on, most of them can't figure out what is happening.

A couple's uniqueness begins with the selection of each other and the traits they bring with them to their interaction. Since many of these factors are unconscious, they account for a certain amount of inexplicable behavior from the outset.

Although couples become couples for the most part because they are *in* love, few can define *love*. They know that it should provide support, gratification, sexual excitement, and spur the fulfilling of their goals—but people often become disappointed in these expectations.

Sometimes this is because they have unconsciously selected (fallen in love with) someone they considered inferior, because they are uncomfortable with the "superior" people they really admire. Sometimes it is because they chose a partner with complementary qualities that changed and ceased to be complementary. For example, a sexually shy and inhibited woman might select a man who is just the opposite. But, secure in the relationship, she may then flower sexually and become as uninhibited as the man. Or, an assertive man may lose patience and finally give up on an inhibited woman and withdraw sexually.

Among the baggage people bring to intimate relationships are unconscious needs to assert or defend themselves, anachronistic feelings about parents, and learned ways of coping that they transfer without critical judgment onto the other person, as well as a variety of anxieties and ways of dealing with them. Any emotion that is unconscious, or conscious but hidden, may serve as a wedge in the relationship, but when it is brought into the open, a couple's interaction is likely to improve.

Unfortunately, there is no single model of how men and women should regard each other, share marital responsibilities, or develop attitudes about monogamy. It requires subtle interplay for two people to be able to respect each other's individuality and create an environment in which both can grow and, at the same time, be in accord. This is what increasing numbers of people have been taught they have a right to expect, and what they want. Yet it is exactly what few are able to achieve or sustain over a long period of time. While we do not understand all the factors that combine to make it so difficult, we do know more than we did even a few years ago.

We can observe, for example, that within a couple, each one adopts a characteristic way of relating to the other. This may shift, depending on the situation but, by and large, the way each relates to the other is his or her personality imprint with this particular lover or mate. With any other, even one who is similar, there will be enough differences to make for different behavior.

The couples you met at the beginning of this chapter all acted in some ways that puzzled them—and they didn't like it. Yet in no case was this isolated behavior; it was habitual, or becoming so, but it was still puzzling, still upsetting. The couples had little control over those feelings or responses. Like them, all of us sometimes act or feel in ways we do not understand, because we have unconscious psychological and biological needs that make us act and feel in alien ways. Even when we are unaware of our needs they help shape our interactions with people—and often cause confusion because we do not understand what is going on.

We have discussed in general terms why many couples are in trouble. What follows will concern you more directly. To minimize your own difficult times and maximize your capacity for loving well, we trust you will find out a good deal here about yourself and the person you love—as well as the way you behave with each other.

2
Behavioral Profiles

Though people interact in an infinite number of ways, for the sake of clarity we have grouped certain characteristic ways into seven major categories and called them *behavioral profiles*. A little familiarity with these categories can give you a degree of insight into patterns of relating between mates and help you to understand some seemingly incomprehensible behavior.

Bear in mind that these profiles are not rigid. Most people, even those who fit a profile well, also show some characteristics of other profiles; moreover, we all shift from one profile to another at different times, possibly even several times in a single day. Making allowances for shifts, choose the profile that most nearly matches the way you behave and the one that best matches your partner's behavior. Look for the characteristics that come closest to the way each of you usually acts with the other. Each profile is described first in general terms, then according to a checklist of behavior based on inner—psychological and biological—needs. Finally, there is a brief illustration of how a person who fits that particular profile might act in a situation; note how easily people can get into trouble because each one seems to be following a secret script. After you read the description, compare your behavior and your partner's to each item on the checklist. It is important to remember that no one will match a profile *exactly,* but only approximately.

EQUAL PARTNERS

Many—but by no means all—people in every part of society now aspire to be equal partners. This desire reflects our new regard for individuality—maintaining one's own strong identity within a close relationship—and for full equality between men and women.

Equal partners want equality for their partners as well as for themselves—even if their partners do not want equality. They expect that both members of the couple will have the same privileges and obligations, devoid of any double standards. They expect that each will be a complete, independent person with his or her own work and friends—but that, at the same time, each will be responsive to the needs of the other. They also expect that, despite other forms of independence, the two will be emotionally interdependent and that each will respect the individuality (including the frailties) of the other.

The equal partner is reasonably able to welcome and tolerate a mature, peer relationship, is relatively noncompetitive with his or her mate, and understands and respects gender differences so that they are never used to either one's disadvantage. An equal partner may at times feel a need to be like a child who wants to be taken care of, and/or act as a parent at times when his or her mate is childlike. These people are flexible. They are relatively free of any continuous urgent need to be catered to like infants; they also realize that they will not be more lovable if they always cater to the infantile needs of the other person.

Checklist of Equal-Partner Behavior Based on Inner Needs

   • Tends to independence; is cooperative and interdependent with mate.
   • Is more active than passive.
   • Is capable of close, sustained intimacy without clinging.
   • Is able to show strength—to share, or assume decision-making

and to allow mate to do the same. Is neither submissive nor dominating. May be competitive with mate, but not destructively so.

• Has no great fear of abandonment.

• Does not seek to possess or to be possessed by mate. Does give, and expect, commitment.

• Has a low to moderate level of anxiety.

• Sexual response to mate varies from moderate to high.

• Has an excellent capacity to love self and mate.

• Has a well-developed and defined style* but also respects mate's.

Sam: Illustration of an Equal Partner in Action

Sam, a true believer in equality, has come to terms with his wife, Lisa, over a fair division of their household chores. They both work outside the home: Sam creatively, as an architect, Lisa in a routine bank job. Since Lisa gets home earlier than Sam, she prepares dinner and cleans up afterward. Sam takes care of the laundry, vacuum-cleaning, and various other tasks.

One evening during dinner Lisa remarks that her favorite television program is now being shown at an earlier hour; she will miss it because she will still be busy in the kitchen when it goes on. Sam immediately says that he has no such conflict with *his* favorite show, and so Lisa should not; he will clean up on Wednesday nights so she can be free. Lisa demurs, but as soon as dinner is over, Sam begins to clear the table and urges Lisa to go watch her program.

To Sam's surprise, Lisa refuses his offer. Not only does she refuse, she is upset and accuses him of meddling. Sam, in turn, feels offended because he was trying to be fair and cannot understand why his gesture was rejected.

Lisa, who has no autonomy in her job, reigns supreme in her kitchen; it is her special domain and she does not want Sam to invade it. But she is no more aware of that than Sam is. She just knows that she feels angry. Sam, for his part, feels puzzled and a little hurt. He shrugs off the incident—but next Wednesday night, he may try

----

* *Style* refers to cognitive style and may be defined as the way people approach and deal with situations and problems. Some like to gather information, then proceed to act logically; others act intuitively or impulsively. Each person has his or her own style in solving problems and in expressing resolutions.

to help again because it appears to him to be the fair thing to do. Perhaps it will dawn on him or Lisa to suggest that she watch her program and clean up later. If either Sam or Lisa were aware of her need to be in charge of her kitchen they could easily reach a happy resolution.

ROMANTIC PARTNER

As equal partnership is the wave of today, romantic partnership is the wave of the most recent past. Even for those who want to be equal, the romantic concept still wields a strong influence. The exciting element of loving closely, and of both people being in harmony all the time, takes precedence for many.

Even if romantics are not as genuinely loving as they think they are, they *act* as if they were. They seem to want—and expect—their partners to be soulmates, to form almost a single entity with them. They act as if they are incomplete and can be whole only together with the loved one.

Since romantics believe that they can be happy solely with another romantic, they become highly vulnerable if the partner refuses to play that role. They try desperately to *make* the partner into a romantic. Often, this becomes an all-absorbing game that the two play: the romantic constantly pushes and tests, the partner pulls back—but carefully, managing to give just enough encouragement to keep the game going. The game provides a good opportunity for complaints about each other:

ROMANTIC: "He (she) isn't sensitive, loving [and so on]."

PARTNER: "He (she) is forever clinging, demanding, always wanting to be with me, trying to make me prove my love."

Romantic partners still pursue the childhood dream of being the sole object of a parent's support, love, even adoration. They look for fulfillment in a partner and almost never have enough evidence of love. However, at such times as they are reasonably secure in a romantic relationship, they can emerge and reach toward their greatest potential.

Because romantics tend to overvalue a partner so extravagantly, they tend to be extremely jealous and protective of the relationship. Love and passion are of major importance, and they often use these emotions like litmus paper to test the quality of the union.

Most romantics fear that the partner will discover something unromantic about them, and they fear the discovery in the partner of something that does not fit their romantic image. More than anything, they want to believe! As a result, they *do*—even if they have to shut out the sound of interior warning bells. But whenever romantics find that a partner is less than they believed, they experience a great sense of betrayal. They claim that the other has changed, or else has been masquerading all along. To an outsider, it is usually clear that the nonromantic mate never behaved as a romantic, had never agreed to—and wouldn't be able to in any case.

Romantics often set great store by sentimental symbols: all anniversaries become important—dates of the first time they met, kissed, had sex together; the songs they shared, places they visited, and so on, assume great meaning.

Checklist of Romantic-Partner Behavior Based on Inner Needs

- Tends to be dependent on mate.
- Is extremely fearful of abandonment, a significant factor in determining behavior.
- Very possessive and controlling, even when appearing to be submissive.
- Has a high level of anxiety; often feels incomplete and incapable of dealing with a hostile world.
- Needs to use many defense mechanisms.*
- May have some mild problems of gender identity.
- Usually has a very intense sexual response to mate.
- Often confuses love with fear of losing mate.
- Style ranges from intuitive to moderately well-organized; usually wants to respect the other's style.

------

* Defense mechanisms are ways people deal with thoughts and perceptions that might make them anxious. Sigmund Freud first described them and their importance in shaping our actions. They are necessary to everyone and we use them positively as well as negatively.

Lisa: Illustration of a Romantic Partner in Action

Lisa and Sam (whom we have just met) are at a cocktail party. They have moved to opposite sides of the room, and Lisa looks up to see Sam in earnest conversation with a woman. She notes that the woman is considerably younger than she, dark-haired, attractive. Lisa instantly wonders whether Sam finds her prettier than she; she remembers having heard him say that brunettes are sexier-looking than blondes.

Later it turns out that the woman is a singer, and she is asked to perform. During the enthusiastic applause that follows, Sam is the first to rush over to praise her performance; he pulls a daisy from his buttonhole and presents it to her.

Lisa is overwhelmed by anguish. *She* had picked that daisy for Sam as they left for the party. She had tucked it into his buttonhole and said "Daisies don't lie. I love you." And now he had given that daisy to another woman! How could he do such a thing?

She tells Sam she has a headache and wants to leave. Sam is perplexed but correctly hears and respects the intensity of her feelings. She begins to cry as soon as they get into the car. By the time they get home she is inconsolable. Sam spends the rest of the evening trying to comfort and reassure her, but it is several days before her distress finally subsides.

PARENTAL PARTNER

A generally descriptive term, a parental partner is no ordinary parent, but one who relates to a mate as if the latter were a child. A parental partner's behavior may range from extremely controlling and authoritative to mildly patronizing and nonaccepting of the other person's desires and judgments.

The prototype of the parental partner is Torvald, Nora's husband in Ibsen's play *A Doll's House*. While Torvald is an extreme case, one who exercises such control over his wife as to maintain her in infant status, some parental partners are benign and loving, and foster the "child's" need for growth and independence up to a point. The script, however, calls for the child's being either so insecure or so masochistic as to continue to play the game of remaining a child, thereby surrendering freedom.

On the other hand, a harsh parental partner may be punitive and authoritarian, expecting the other person to play the role of an obedient child. If the childlike one threatens to upset the status quo, the parental one becomes even more demanding in an effort to maintain control.

In either case, the essence of the relationship is that the parental one is able to feel adult by acting as parent to an accepting child-partner. The parent's word is law, and transgressions can be tolerated only as the foolish acts of an irresponsible child, who may be forgiven by the benevolent, patronizing adult. This elaborate system serves as a defense against the parental partner's underlying lack of self-esteem.

The parent has little real interest in the child's growing up and making decisions. Small projects of one sort or another may be encouraged—taking an adult-education course, for example—but they are approved only as long as the parental partner can see them as the equivalent of opening a lemonade stand by the side of a quiet road. If the childlike partner attempts serious study, new and more challenging work, or any other true threat to the status quo, the parental partner may engage in subtle sabotage or even show outright fear and rage.

One kind of parental partner seeks out those who need to be "saved"; the "rescuer" feels superior to a weak and childish person who needs to be saved from a bad life situation—parents' home, bad marriage, poverty, alcoholism, drug abuse, poor health, or whatever. If the relationship continues, he or she remains the parental partner; if it dissolves, a new victim of adversity is sought. As long as he or she keeps saving people, the rescuer feels secure in someone's love because he or she feels needed.

Checklist of Parental-Partner Behavior Based on Inner Needs

- Tends to be somewhat independent, but may be very dependent on the other's remaining childlike; will go to great lengths to keep him or her that way.
- Tends to be more active than passive.
- Needs to be powerful, to dominate mate. Is competitive and must constantly demonstrate own superior competence.
- Has a great fear of abandonment. Cannot afford to lose mate.
- Has a great need to possess and control, although ultimately a childlike partner often has greater control.
- Usually tends to be sexually responsive.
- Deprecates or patronizes mate's style. Own style is well organized and leads to prompt problem-solving.

Dick: Illustration of a Parental Partner in Action

Dick's new wife, Pat, came to the city from a farm community right after she graduated from high school. She worked as a secretary until her marriage, but now she divides her time between caring for their home, learning to bake, and preparing her daily lessons for Dick. Himself an accomplished linguist, Dick has been giving Pat Spanish and French lessons every evening in preparation for a projected trip to Europe.

Pat has little aptitude for language; she confuses the two languages hopelessly, can pronounce neither the French nor the Spanish *r,* and cannot for the life of her get the hang of agreement between nouns and adjectives. But Dick finds her errors charming, laughs gaily with her over each one, and clearly enjoys the lessons. There are other lessons, too. Pat cannot balance her checkbook, keep the household accounts straight, or understand which receipts have to be saved for tax records. Dick keeps on explaining.

But he is somewhat less patient about some other matters. He constantly reprimands her for leaving her clothes strewn about and letting food turn moldy in the refrigerator. Each time he scolds she promises to try to do better.

Pat has recently suggested that maybe it would be better if she returned to work and used her salary to pay for a housekeeper, but Dick is strenuously opposed to the idea; every time she raises the subject, he stops criticizing her for several days.

CHILDLIKE PARTNER

The childlike partner is the counterpart of the parental partner. This person *wants* to be the child in the relationship and, if possible, may maneuver the other person into playing parent. Childlike partners want to be taken care of, protected, guided, and disciplined. In exchange, they offer a mate the right to feel adult and needed, and like real children, may afford much joy and gladness.

Again like real children, these partners may become powerful; their power derives from the parental person's need to have a child, in order to feel like an adult. Most childlike partners are aware of this and sometimes exploit the situation by threatening to leave. Although this kind of match is common in man-woman couples, it is particularly clearly seen in homosexual relationships in which the parental partner often lives in fear of losing the controlling child partner.

Nearly all men and women retain some remnants of childhood dependence no matter how much competence they achieve; it is the ability to bring forth the creative child in one's self that others generally find charming. However, the childlike creativity and playfulness that we display on occasion is not to be confused with the full-time dependence and pseudo-innocence that the childlike partner adopts with his or her mate.

Checklist of Childlike-Partner Behavior Based on Inner Needs

- Tends to be dependent.
- Is largely passive.
- Does not seek much power and generally submits to partner. May, however, use power (threaten to withdraw or leave) to dominate when mate is emotionally dependent.
- Has a great fear of abandonment which often motivates behavior.
- Has a high level of anxiety.
- Requires many defense mechanisms.
- Sexual response to mate is positive to enthusiastic.
- Style is somewhat chaotic and intuitive. Often ridicules partner's more organized style, but deeply appreciates its benefits.

Pat: Illustration of a Childlike Partner in Action

Pat (the childlike partner of parental Dick) was thrilled with her marriage and the opportunity to have given up her job; in fact, she wasn't very competent at the job and felt (correctly) that she would soon be fired. She has genuine admiration for Dick's knowledge and ability to run things. Her only complaint is that she wishes he would get off her back about her sloppy ways. She knows intuitively, however, that all she has to do is threaten to go back to work and she can twist him around her little finger.

RATIONAL PARTNER

Rational partners cannot admit that emotions may influence behavior. They try to establish reasoned, logical, well-ordered relationships and to delineate clearly all duties within the partnership; they always fulfill their responsibilities and cannot comprehend why the other person does not do likewise. Each failure of the mate to pull her or his weight calls forth a patient, logical explanation of what should be done. This implacable logic often annoys the other person and triggers sharp reactions.

Although rational partners do not usually demonstrate much overt affection or passion, they are capable of deep feelings of love and experience great pain if they lose someone they love. They tend to have a bookkeeping approach to the details of life, with every item in the proper column, and every column neatly tallied. They are pragmatic, down-to-earth; they understand the system they live by and play the game of life according to set rules. They rarely attempt to change those rules or to create new ones. Although they assume their own correctness in all matters of a factual nature, they often defer to their mate in matters of taste, style, and culture.

Understandably, rational partners provoke anger in some mates, even those who want limits set for themselves. The rational partner is then blamed for being "so *damned* rational," for not being more of a free spirit—but all the while he or she is willingly being maneuvered into taking over and being extremely responsible.

Rational partners often exhibit social grace, kindness, and consideration, and are usually there when needed—even though they may not appear to be sensitive to all the nuances of their mate's feelings. They may, if the dynamics are right, slip over into becoming parental partners. This behavior is apt to be elicited when a mate plays out the role of helpless child, unable to deal with life's complexities.

Once committed, a rational partner tends to be loyal and devoted to making the relationship work. An apparent lack of sensitivity to the other partner's emotional needs may cause some disharmony, but the relationship is often a close and intimate one. In any case, the essential behavior is to appear to make decisions by cool logic, while the balance sheet is always being automatically updated. Unless the rational partner's mate leaves, the two of them may never fully realize how truly interdependent they are.

Checklist of Rational-Partner Behavior Based on Inner Needs

- Often more dependent than is apparent. Forms close and emotionally dependent relationships but hides many emotional needs and remains in charge of the practical, administrative side of the relationship.
- While very active in practical matters, leaves to mate those aspects of their common existence that have greater emotional content. There is, therefore, a division of responsibilities that may or may not be satisfactory.
- Can be quite close, but tends to avoid deep, continued expressions of motivation and analysis of feelings; may actually be distant and removed.
- Tends to assume and use power and to appear dominant. Often, however, appearance is deceptive and the mate has the ultimate power. Usually not competitive with partner.
- Is well defended against fear of abandonment.
- Anxiety level is low, rarely exceeding average.
- Generally capable of a deep and lasting love relationship.
- Own style is highly organized; collects all data, then arrives at "correct" and logical conclusions. Expects others to conform to these conclusions because they are "obviously right." Not likely to accept any other style except in a condescending way.

Max: Illustration of a Rational Partner in Action

Max and his partner, Gloria, are on a sightseeing tour. Max has made all the arrangements. Each hotel has been chosen with infinite care because it has the best location, the most charm, or the best food in the area; trains, planes, and car rentals have been reserved for each day of the trip. Max has typed up two copies, one for Gloria, one for himself, of a daily itinerary that includes every place they will visit, how long they will stay, what they will see, where they will dine, what time they will leave and by what means. Max has gone to a great deal of trouble and is pleased with the plans he has worked out.

Gloria runs into problems with the schedule almost daily: She washes her hair at the last minute and they miss their plane; she isn't hungry and can't eat when the itinerary calls for lunch at a delightful inn; she is famished when they are still two hours from their next stop; she finds some of the stops boring and wants to go on, loves others and wants to stay an extra day. Each time she raises an objection, Max explains carefully why they must adhere to the schedule. By the time the trip is half over, Gloria tells him that if he so much as mentions the schedule one more time, she will catch the next plane for home.

Max cannot understand Gloria's reaction and feels confused and hurt after he has gone to so much trouble to plan this delightful trip for both of them.

COMPANIONATE PARTNER

Companionate partners act primarily to ward off being alone. They can usually accept closeness without expecting love. They do seek thoughtfulness and kindness and believe in their own willingness to give the same in return—perhaps with financial security as well.

Essentially, companionate partners want someone with whom to share day-to-day living, and they readily accept the necessary give and take involved. While they may deeply desire romantic love, they do not work toward it; some companionate people might be described as "retired romantics."

A companionate-partner arrangement can be a good one for those who no longer measure a relationship against some abstract ideal. It has become increasingly popular, with or without marriage, among older couples; they see it as a realistic arrangement between people who no longer have illusions, who know what their needs are and what they are willing to give up to have them satisfied.

The companionate partner's style is based on genuine deep needs combined with acceptable compromises. These people enter into relationships because they do not want to be alone, not because they are desperately driven by a fear of loneliness. They do not expect a passionate love relationship.

Checklist of Companionate-Partner Behavior Based on Inner Needs

- Often shows a mixture of independence and dependence without an extreme amount of either.
- Tends to be somewhat more active than passive.
- Is neither very close nor very distant.
- Exercises power, but moderately. Usually not competitive.
- Prefers life with a partner, but has no great fear of abandonment.
- Love in the usual sense, which includes passion, is of no great importance, but acceptance, need, commitment, and kindness are essential.
- Style tends to be well-ordered and rational. Can accept mate's style if it does not undergo (or seem to undergo) change.

Betty: Illustration of a Companionate Partner in Action

Betty was widowed some years ago after a long, happy marriage. While able to live alone and to function well enough, she found single life simply not much fun; there seemed no point in going on a trip alone, and even a movie seemed worthless when there was no one to discuss it with afterward. Accustomed to good communication with her late husband, Betty missed the give and take across the dining table, gossip after a party, the lively interchange that followed reading a new book.

On a visit to her home town, Betty met Albert, a man she and her husband had known long before. Albert had now been divorced for two years, and he was delighted to meet Betty again. He took her to dinner several times, and the night before she left confessed that he had loved her from afar for many years, still did, and hoped she would consider marrying him.

Betty liked Albert but found him a little dull; he lacked the wit, originality, and *joie de vivre* of her late husband. She could not avoid the comparison. But he had a number of good qualities. He was a kind, considerate man with a gentle disposition; he liked to travel, was a good conversationalist, and was reasonably intelligent. Betty was not in love with him and knew that she never would be. At the same time, she believed he would be pleasant to live with and that their life together would be an improvement over life alone. She agreed to the marriage with little hesitation.

PARALLEL PARTNER

The parallel partner avoids an intimate, sharing relationship. Despite any protests to the contrary, he or she needs emotional distance and independence, and wants a mate who will respect that need. The need for distance may be a generalized defense against the anxiety that intimacy triggers or simply a response to a particular partner or a combination of both.

Parallel partners like all the conventional trappings of marriage— a home, children, a dog, slippers, a washing machine—without intimacy. They prefer separate beds or bedrooms, sometimes even separate residences. Figuratively speaking, they like fingertip touch better than a full embrace. They "share" children, will go to social, community, and family functions with a partner, but the two are not close.

Nothing is more important to parallel partners than maneuvering a mate so that the two can keep a necessary, comfortable distance. They struggle against being merged in any way, for fear of losing integrity and of being controlled. The defensive makeup of parallel partners is emphatically demonstrated by their emotional distance. Although they appear to be cool and guarded people, they may be extremely charming.

A parallel partner's need for distance is often a defense against a dependency need so great that it cannot consciously be acknowledged. If the defense were ever penetrated, the parallel partner might well melt into a romantic with an extreme need for a mate who would insure "completion"; he or she would then be excruciatingly vulnerable to that partner—an outcome to be avoided at all costs. The costs include this eternal struggle against emotional involvement.

Checklist of Parallel-Partner Behavior Based on Inner Needs

• Tends to be somewhat independent and doesn't mind if mate is. The important thing is that mate must be able to respect the basic ground rule of emotional distance.

• Is generally more active than passive.

• Is incapable of sustained closeness.

• Tends to be in charge of himself or herself and of setting the fundamental style of the relationship. Prefers mate to have power in his or her own areas of daily life and work. Is usually not very competitive.

• Has an intense fear of abandonment, but is well guarded against it by the defense of maintaining distance.

• On one level, does not want to possess or be possessed; on another, must exert extreme control to keep mate from violating the requisite distance boundary.

• Sexual response to mate varies, but, when intense, it is usually on a purely physical level with few admitted emotional components. Can be a technically competent but otherwise ungiving sexual partner.

• No great love of self or mate since love must be inhibited. Is commonly narcissistic.

• Tends to be fairly well organized and to have a rigid style. Is rarely able to incorporate mate's style to complement his or her own, since that would require closeness.

Paul: Illustration of a Parallel Partner in Action

Paul is nearly forty and has never been married, although he has had several long alliances. The last one, with Diane, is typical. The two met at a convention nearly three years ago, and Diane, a divorcée with a young daughter, was charmed by Paul. They dated with increasing frequency for several months, finally agreed that they would both stop seeing other people. Soon Paul began to spend weekends at Diane's apartment, and Diane's daughter Nancy accepted him as a fact of life. Paul grew very fond of the child and frequently took her to the zoo, a museum, or to special events such as the circus. He seemed genuinely to enjoy life as a member of the family, and spoke often of "when we're married."

Finally, Diane began to press for a wedding date. Her apartment lease was coming up for renewal, her family and friends kept asking what they were waiting for, and her former husband was grumbling about the effects of the arrangement on Nancy. Paul was willing to discuss the kind of wedding they would have, where they might go on a wedding trip, where they would live—but he couldn't be pinned down to a date. He was sympathetic to the problem of Diane's lease but he had innumerable reasons for urging that they maintain the status quo for the time being: he had too many books to move; he needed a quiet place to work; his apartment, while too small for the three of them, was close to his office; and so on.

Paul and Diane still weekend together. They entertain as a couple, go out as a couple, and share a beach house in the summer. But after three years, Diane is about at the end of her rope. She has recently gone into therapy, and although Paul doesn't know it yet, she will probably soon decide to give him up.

3

Easy-and Uneasy-Alliances

The preceding chapter gave you a glimpse of the basic ways people behave with each other and the chance to identify the profiles closest to your own and your partner's.

Each profile included an illustration of how a specific person behaves in a specific relationship; the quality of a partnership depends on *both* members' profiles and the way they act together. That interaction is what we are going to consider in this chapter.

Some partnership combinations are "naturals"—a parental partner and a childlike one, for example. But, similarly, there are *un*natural combinations that are poor fits, and the mismatched couple is likely to fall on hard times unless they can change something.

Some relationships do a good job of serving the needs of both mates, but others fail miserably. And while all relationships change, some are more stable than others. The ones that gratify tend to last; those that do not gratify are susceptible to hostility, increasing distance, and /or eventual dissolution.

It is not possible to discuss every kind of partnership combination, but this chapter describes the major ones in broad outline. As with the behavioral profiles, do not expect to find exact blueprints of yourselves or of couples you know. These descriptions merely sketch the basic ways in which partners interact.

EQUAL-PARTNER COMBINATIONS

Equal-Equal

There is no model for couple behavior so popular today as the equal-equal one. By now, you need not be a trend-setter, a feminist, or an intellectual to follow the model, in part or completely. You may be following this model even if you have never thought or talked about it—or, on the other hand, you might think and talk about it a great deal but find it hard to enact. The fact is that while a large number of contemporary couples *want* equality, not many find it easy to achieve. No one can simply will it. A couple can maintain it only if they have deep and genuine respect for themselves and for each other. Simple? Well, not very. It probably would be if we didn't all come equipped with histories—but we do. Virtually all of us were brought up to believe that men and women were meant to play sharply different, and unequal, roles in life. Unless we have unlearned most of what we were so carefully taught, we have some ambivalence about equality. If we're slightly ambivalent, it doesn't hurt too much. But if we're moderately or strongly ambivalent, then a truly equal relationship does not come easily; we have to struggle for it every step of the way. That's what a large number of couples are doing now, and with the best will in the world; they are able to *act* equal but they don't really *feel* equal.

Another thing that makes equal-equal combinations difficult is that even when they are good, they can founder more easily than many other kinds of relationship. It isn't that equal partners don't take their relationships seriously. They do. But if one of them falls out of love or gets involved with someone else, the consequences are likely to be swifter and more drastic than for others. The reason: People who are able to be truly egalitarian are people who are secure. Their security keeps them from walking away without good cause, but that same security makes it possible for them to leave a relationship that is no longer loving, rewarding, or conducive to growth. They are not immobilized by the fear of being alone or of starting over. Equal partners stay together because they want to, not —like many others—because they are afraid not to.

Of course, this has its very good side, too. Equal-equal partners can enjoy long and gratifying lives together after the first flush of their passion is ended. They rarely find each other dull, and they never experience the flatness that creeps into the relationships of peace-at-any-price mates who stick together out of inertia or fear of the unknown. Equal partners are not afraid to compete with or challenge each other, and they don't avoid an argument when it's necessary to resolve an issue; it doesn't make them nervous to rock the boat.

They aren't afraid of public opinion, either. Many other couples are held together by a variety of outside forces—children, family, friends, church, and so on. But equal partners are secure enough to be independent of others, and they don't do what's expected of them if it isn't what they want to do.

And because they are secure, equal partners don't have to "own" each other. They believe that each person should be free to function separately. Each has the status and identification that derive from his or her own activities, not the partner's. No equal woman wants to be known as So-and-So's wife, no matter how important he may be. If her husband *is* prominent, she may not be able to avoid being known as his wife—but she would much prefer to be recognized for who *she* is, and what she does, and she will make every effort to achieve this recognition.

Equal partners don't feel that they always have to do the same thing at the same time. In the last century it was shocking for a husband and wife to make separate social appearances, but in today's society it is no longer unusual. In some circles, even separate sexual relationships are tolerated if that's what the couple wants—but extramarital sexual activities are not by any means a sign of equality.

Within those equal relationships that function well, different couples achieve their goals by different means. They hold a variety of basic beliefs that reflect many of the philosophies of our time. One has to do with role definition.

There are equal-equal partners who believe that men and women should break away from the confinement of performing only those tasks that tradition has labeled *male* or *female,* and should share all of them equally. The men do half the housework, cooking, shopping, child rearing, and the like. The women earn money, take equal responsibility for home repairs, yard work, financial decisions, and so on. The two act together to settle all questions that affect them both and never make important decisions unilaterally.

But there are other equal partners—and these are just as equal—who favor some well-defined gender roles along traditional lines. They believe that family life is more successful when men and women do assume different tasks, but that neither person's tasks are more demeaning or creative than the other's. True equality here is based not on the kind of work the two do, but on their respect for each other's individuality and contributions. A woman who cares for the home and children does a job that is just as important as any man's —in truth, it may be far more creative, and she knows it. She is not expected to take a turn at changing the oil in the car or repairing a leaky toilet—unless, of course, she wants to. And she doesn't expect her mate to understand the intricacies of separating the delicate-cycle laundry from the rest of the heap or to cook dinner for company— unless those are things he particularly likes to do. Neither is forced into a unisex Procrustean bed; each chooses the responsibilities he or she does best and feels comfortable with. In such relationships partners play more or less conventional roles, but see to it that each has ample opportunity for growth.

Another set of philosophical variations centers around money. For some equal-equal partners, literal economic equality is basic—but attaining equality is difficult.

There are only three ways for a woman to be economically secure: (1) through her ability to earn as much as a man would in the same job—i.e., at least a living wage; (2) through marriage to a man who earns enough to support her; and (3) through inheritance. Unfortunately, each one of these routes has a built-in flaw. First, although the women's movement has certainly spurred more job opportunities for women, they have not achieved equality in terms of equal pay for equal work. And equal work is hard to find; most women's jobs are still clustered in lower-level areas such as clerical, service, and retail sales. Second, even if a woman's husband supports her in fine style, as long as she has no income of her own she often feels (or is told that she *should* feel) less than a complete person. Her status comes from her husband's position instead of her own, and her sense of self is often impaired. As for the final means—inheritance—it falls to so few that it does not even justify discussion here.

How, then, are we to deal with the lack of economic equality between men and women? Only about half of all married women work, and of those who do about 10 percent earn more than their husbands, while another 10 percent earn roughly the same amount; for the great majority, the solution cannot depend on equal earning power. There is a solution, however, and a simple one: a couple's attitude and approach to the entire matter of money. Consider these two cases, both of which involve married women who stay at home.

Lou Selby is a mechanic. Angela, his wife, left her secretarial job a year after their wedding, shortly before their first child was born. Now, eight years later, that child is in the third grade, and her younger brother, four, won't start kindergarten until next year. Although the Selbys made much of being an egalitarian couple during their first year of marriage, they began to change their habits after the baby came. At first the changes were subtle, but by now the couple operate very differently from the way they began.

Lou has an exhausting job and usually comes home tired. He does play with the children for a few minutes as soon as he gets in, but right after dinner is over, he sinks into his easy chair to read the paper or watch a television show. Angela never asks him to help with the dishes or the children's bath any more because she thinks it would be unfair. Lou has to get up early in the morning. He puts in a hard day at work, even volunteers for overtime to make a little extra money—and he doesn't leave part of it at the corner pub the way some of his friends do. Angela appreciates what he does and believes that he deserves relaxation in the evening. Which means that the housework and children are her responsibility and hers alone—and that she has no free time for herself.

She often feels a little guilty when she catches herself wishing that she were back at her old job. Her boss thought highly of her; she was good at her work and she was *somebody* at the office. Although she is a good housekeeper and mother, too, this kind of work does not attract much praise or even notice. Angela misses being appreciated—and she misses her paycheck even more, especially when she sees some little luxury she would love to buy but doesn't want to ask Lou for the extra money. Not that Lou is stingy. It's just that he works so hard to provide and to put a little something away each week for the children's college tuitions; he keeps a special account for the purpose. Angela feels that it's only right for her to get along on what Lou gives her, even though it means doing without things she would like to have. And while she still tells herself that she is an equal partner, Angela doesn't feel very equal any more.

The Flanagans are a couple who appear to be much like the Selbys. They are about the same age, have two children, and Janet, like Angela, quit her job to raise a family. Mark is a salesman and has roughly the same income as Lou.

But there the resemblance ends. Janet's image of herself and of her role in marriage is thoroughly different from Angela's. Since she had always planned to go back to work when both children were in school, Janet has been preparing herself for a new career right along. She goes to the nearby community college every Tuesday and Thursday night and will have her certificate next spring. Mark hurries home on her school nights to give the children their dinner and put them to bed. By the time Janet gets back, the kids are asleep, the kitchen is clean, and Mark has a pot of tea or a glass of wine ready for her arrival.

Unlike Angela, Janet doesn't have to ask Mark for money if she wants to buy something special. Even though Mark is the only breadwinner at present, it's because that is his major task, just as taking care of the home and children is Janet's; both partners feel that they make equal contributions. As a result, the money that Mark earns doesn't belong to him, but to him and Janet equally. The Flanagans have a joint bank account, Janet knows what all their financial obligations are, and she feels as free as Mark to spend money.

Even though Janet has not worked at an outside job for a number of years, she has never lost her sense of equality. The Flanagans have, by and large, divided the tasks along traditional lines as the Selbys have, but there are two important differences: They are more flexible in their roles (Mark takes over Janet's chores when necessary and Janet is preparing to share the financial burden). And the fact that Mark presently earns all the income doesn't make him boss over the money or Janet. Unlike the Selbys, the Flanagans have an equal-equal marriage.

Whether or not a married (or otherwise partnered) woman works, it is generally advantageous to both members of the couple if they can establish a sense of economic equality. A grown woman who has to ask for money feels like a child and is usually consciously or unconsciously resentful and demeaned by it; she and the partnership suffer. If she co-manages the funds, she still may be secretly or overtly dissatisfied about some things, but money probably will not be one of them.

Beyond finances, different people often expect different things from their equal relationships. As we have already seen, individuals have different criteria for equality, and two definitions of the word within one couple can be a source of friction. Sometimes the entire concept of equality is spurious: it may be used as a smoke screen to cover up a desire to be taken care of, a fear of responsibility, or a sense of inadequacy.

Not that there is anything wrong with having such fears as long as we recognize them; anxieties like these are normal for both men and women. It would be unreasonable to suppose that we all developed in the same way or according to the same timetable. Because we did not, we are "advanced" or "mature" in one area, "childlike" or "infantile" in another.

People commonly challenge their mates with "You can't have it both ways." When a woman says this, she often means "You can't expect me to hold down a job and still cook, clean, and iron your shirts the way your mother did." And when a man says it, he often means "You can't expect to compete with men in your job, compete with me on the tennis court, compete with everyone in political discussions, and then pull that itsy-poo-feminine-wiles stuff."

But why not? Why *can't* they have it both ways? Everyone *wants* to—and even when we don't get it, we keep trying. We all want the best of whatever is new—but we're all products of our own time, of our families, and have brought our cultural heritages along with us right into contemporary times. None of it balances out quite perfectly, and trying to be equal partners in an unequal world is a complex challenge.

It can become decidedly more complex (or at the very least, different) when only one partner is equality-minded, which isn't unusual. Equality is an elastic concept, and while to some people equal means absolutely equal, others are quite satisfied to have partners who are a little less equal than they are.

Equal-Romantic

This combination can be a good one provided neither partner expects the other to change. As soon as they try to control each other, they are likely to run into as much trouble as Rosanne, an equal partner who lives with Luke, a romantic partner.

Luke needs a great deal of togetherness and as long as he and Rosanne could spend all their nonworking time together, their relationship flourished. But then Rosanne's company began to send her to out-of-town sales conferences that kept her away for several days at a time. Luke was brave while the first separation was still impending, but the day Rosanne left he became acutely anxious. He called her hotel several times during the evening, then started to feel frantic because she was not in her room. By the time he finally reached her, he was in great distress; it didn't help matters for Rosanne to tell him with enthusiasm that she was having a marvelous time. Luke phoned twice more that same night—once just after Rosanne had fallen asleep—and when she complained about being awakened, he became furious with her for "deserting" him and having a good time while he was in anguish.

A few months later, as the next sales meeting approached, Rosanne urged Luke not to stay home alone, depressed and desolate, but to make plans for the nights she would be away; she suggested that he have dinner with friends or buy tickets for a play or a concert. But Luke said that he couldn't possibly enjoy anything without Rosanne and urged her to stay home—even suggesting that she quit her job if necessary.

Now it was Rosanne's turn to feel threatened and angry, and by the time she left for the airport, the pair were barely speaking. After another year of this kind of struggle, they separated.

Fortunately, Rosanne and Luke are an extreme case. Most equal partners have a dash of the romantic—and many romantics subscribe to some aspects of equality; they may even be romantic about the whole idea of equality. And so, if neither partner is too rigid or too anxiety-ridden, an equal-romantic combination may be a happy one.

Equal-Rational

This is often a good combination because the rational partner is trying hard to to be equal and to keep the relationship going. When equal-rational partners run into serious trouble, it is often for reasons like these:

Carl and Amanda had started out as equal-equal partners, but after Carl joined a health club and a bridge club, activities that Amanda had neither the time nor the inclination to share, they began to change. Carl's frequent absences struck Amanda as irresponsible, thoughtless, even irrational. She tried constantly, in patient detailed discussions, to point out that although she was meticulously aware of Carl's needs, schedules, and feelings, he was not at all concerned with hers. She seemed always to have three or four excellent reasons why it was important for Carl to be home whenever he planned to be somewhere else: she had counted on having guests to dinner; it was his sister's birthday and they ought to drop by to deliver her gift; she had thought he would go with her to the tenants' meeting; it was blood-drive night and she had signed them both up for donations.

Amanda genuinely believed herself to be an equal partner. She certainly *wanted* to be one—but she couldn't stand Carl's independence. The more independent he became, the more anxious she became. Although she had little notion of it, her repeated efforts to keep Carl home were really attempts to still her anxiety, and all the other reasons she gave were only incidental. But she never ran out of reasons, and they were invariably rational and logical ones.

Unfortunately, the more Amanda tried to keep Carl home the more he wanted to go out, and the worse her anxiety became. By now they both find the situation intolerable and are engaged in a bitter battle. They recognize what is happening although they have no idea why. Aside from Carl's outside hobbies, they still seem to agree about most things and don't have many specific complaints about each other. Yet if they don't soon find out what lies behind their problem, it will be too late.

But more often, an equal-rational couple will be more like this one:

Olga, a rational partner, has a perfect complement in her friend, Dan; he is able to supply the emotion and spontaneity she is afraid to experience personally. Dan, an equal partner, is sometimes a romantic lover, often a playful child—but always he is warm and loving. Since Olga cannot express love directly, she basks in Dan's warmth and affection.

For his part, Dan often wishes that Olga could be more emotional or imaginative, but he understands her and appreciates her many fine qualities. She may be earthbound, but she is also steadfast and loyal. If she and Dan marry they will do well together as long as Dan does nothing to disappoint or injure her.

To varying degrees, equal partners can accommodate several other kinds of partners as long as their own freedom isn't curtailed or threatened too much. There are some with whom they generally do badly. Here are a few highlights of other combinations:

Equal-Companionate

May work very well. Biggest trouble area: Equal wants more love than Companionate can give; or Equal wants a more independent partner than Companionate can be. Companionate grows angry over demands and anxious over the realization that Equal *is* independent and less than enthusiastic about having a dependent partner.

Equal-Parallel

Sometimes works out well—as long as Equal doesn't demand too much intimacy. Parallel's distance spurs Equal on to try to get closer, and Parallel has to move farther away. The contest may make for a lively relationship—or may destroy it. Equal may eventually give up because the desired quality of love is not forthcoming.

Equal-Parental

Unstable combination. Parental *must* be dominating—but Equal doesn't like to be dominated, and doesn't want a parent.

Equal-Childlike

Also unstable. Equal doesn't want to take care of a child, but does want a love relationship with an adult worthy of respect. Childlike tries—often ingeniously—to force parenthood on Equal, but it's a losing game.

ROMANTIC-PARTNER COMBINATIONS

Romantic-Romantic

At first blush, it looks as if a romantic does best with another romantic; they fit together like two pieces of a puzzle: fragments alone, but together a whole. Sometimes indeed they are that, and fare well over a long period of years. These are the lucky ones, not the majority.

The secret of their success lies in their ability to fill each other's needs even though each of them is so needy: these people can be equally supportive or dependent, and can easily shift back and forth when a situation requires it. They can shift power back and forth, too, but never in such a way that either one becomes dominant over the other. The main thing here is that the couple manages always to act as a unit.

Romantics in this kind of successful relationship don't suffer from anxiety over being abandoned since they both feel secure and thoroughly loved. The biggest fear each has is that the other one will die first. While they have assorted problems, as all couples do, they can generally cope with whatever comes along and remain together throughout life.

Some romantics create a snug and cozy world of their own; they have innumerable secrets—words, symbols with special meanings, names that are theirs alone. They are surrounded by a private environment that they do not share with anyone else.

Married couples of this sort sometimes elect to remain childless; the presence of a child in their own precious sphere would be tantamount to an invasion. In *Cat's Cradle* (1963), Kurt Vonnegut, Jr., beautifully described a pair of romantics, the Mintons, who . . . "entertained each other endlessly with little gifts: sights worth seeing out the plane window, amusing or instructive bits from things they read, random recollections of things gone by." The account goes on to characterize this relationship as one in which the Mintons exist to give each other's lives significance—and in the end, they die within a week of each other.

But in real life, not all romantic-romantic partners fall into a pattern of long-term bonded bliss. For the great majority, the passion, openness, intimacy, and pervasive interdependence of the first few years tend to run down hill after a while, as it did with the Gordons.

Ruth and Jake thought of themselves as soulmates when they married four years ago. They spoke a kind of elaborate baby talk when they were alone and called each other by such pet names as "Dove," "Ducky," "Sweetie." They held hands and cried quiet tears whenever they heard the slow movement of Tchaikovsky's Fifth Symphony; they read aloud to each other from the romantic poets (they were particularly fond of Elizabeth Barrett Browning), wrote each other long love letters (even though they were never separated for a single day), and they had guests only when absolutely necessary because they loathed having anyone else around to spoil their idyllic privacy.

But then Ruth bumped into an old friend who had just been divorced, and brought her home to dinner. The woman was in touch with some of Ruth's other girlhood chums and Ruth thought it would be fun to see them again. She planned a little party, and soon she and Jake were dining back and forth with a whole group of (to Jake) extraneous people. He could not understand why Ruth preferred these social evenings to their quiet twosomes. She seemed changed. And she was changing in other ways, too. She didn't use their private words much any more, and they hadn't read poetry to each other in a month. Ruth seemed busy, distracted—not the soulmate she used to be. It was an impossible thought, but it struck Jake that his wife no longer loved him.

And so he set about trying to woo her back to the old footing. He sent her eight red roses (one for every way of loving in "How do I love thee . . ."), wrote her several long, passionate letters, played Tchaikovsky nightly, called her by all the special endearing names they had ever used—but she didn't respond. If anything, she grew even more remote.

Jake didn't know what had happened to Ruth (he still doesn't) but there are several possibilities. She might have developed into an equal, a parallel, or a companionate partner. Or Jake may have crossed the line from romantic to childlike so that his behavior now strikes Ruth as overly dependent. Or, perhaps he is the same, and Ruth may be as romantic as ever but needs a brand-new romantic relationship so that she can reexperience the intense romantic passion and intimacy she had with Jake in the early years. In any case, he senses that Ruth is slipping away from him—and he's right. When she goes, he will be so bereaved that he will not consider life worth living. He will vow never to love anyone again—and in fact, he may never love again in the same intense way. If, after a long period of healing and restoration, he does select another mate, it might be to establish a companionate relationship, one without passion or closeness.

Many romantic-romantic partners are less extreme than Jake and Ruth were, and don't become "soulmates" to the same extent. They do, however, always feel that they need each other in order to be complete, and any time one of them tries to create a little more space, the other is likely to tighten the loving bonds too much, as Jake did. But when romantic partners are at their best, even though they have an interlocked relationship, they are able to free each other enough to function productively and survive as a couple.

Romantic-Rational

Often difficult, but not impossible. Romantic feels that Rational should be closer, more expressive, more sentimental, less logical. Relationship may survive because of an underlying subrelationship of child-parent that both find rewarding. Even while berating Rational for shortcomings, Romantic can feel superior for being so much more "sensitive." Rational can accept complaints with relative calm by feeling like a good parent indulging a whimsical child.

Romantic-Companionate

Often a former romantic-romantic combination that made the transition when one of the partners cooled down. If Romantic can really accept the change, they may survive as a brother-sister or parent-child couple. But if Romantic makes a strong effort to reestablish the old relationship, Companionate may withdraw completely.

Romantic-Parallel

Very unstable since Romantic cannot stand Parallel's distance. Sometimes, however, Romantic in this combination may not be a true romantic, but a pseudoromantic who cannot tolerate too much closeness either, and so the two play an unconscious game. Romantic insists the relationship isn't warm enough, thereby forcing Parallel to move farther away—except for a sudden gesture of closeness to keep Romantic whenever the latter is ready to leave. Romantic then continues to complain, Parallel moves for distance again, and the game goes on.

Romantic-Parental

May work well. Romantic can easily fall into a childlike stance—as long as Parent is not too demanding. Then it's a good complementary relationship for both.

Romantic-Childlike

Poor. Romantics have a tendency to be childlike themselves and grow uneasy without a "grownup." A little childishness is fun, but more than a little is too much.

PARENTAL-PARTNER COMBINATIONS

Parental-Childlike

A parental partner needs a child; a child needs a parent. When two partners interact so as to play these complementary roles without ambivalence, they can have a very good relationship. Sam and Marion are a case in point.

The first time Sam ever saw Marion was between the halves of a high school football game. She was the captain of the cheerleading squad and Sam was instantly captivated by her exuberance and energy as well as by her dimples and flashing smile. He arranged to meet her right after the game, and on their first date he nicknamed her "Baby Doll"—a name that lasted right into their marriage four years later.

Marion really was more baby doll than woman. She was charming, full of fun, and generally ready to do anything Sam wanted to do. But she was spectacularly poor at running the house, handling simple accounts, or even answering mail. At first Sam thought it was charming that Marion was so helpless in the kitchen; he never tired of telling how she had boiled the lettuce and made salad of the cabbage leaves. Later, when he had had his fill of inedible meals, he frequently took a hand in the dinner preparations and they often ate out.

Marion's checking account was regularly overdrawn until Sam established the habit of sitting down with her checkbook once or twice a month to straighten out the balance. There were always financial crises anyway, because Marion seemed to mislay the bills; they sometimes came to Sam's attention only when threats to discontinue service or collection-agency letters arrived.

The social calendar proved as hazardous as the checkbook for Marion, and on a few occasions she and Sam forgot to go to dinner parties, turned up on the wrong night, and once weren't home when their own invited guests arrived. So Sam took over the engagement calendar, too.

How does he feel about assuming responsibility for all these extra chores? Well, after the initial charm wore off, he grumbled a lot—but the fact is that Marion is a perfect wife for him. Deep down inside, Sam doesn't feel very lovable—and as long as Marion can't get along without him, he knows he is safe. She *needs* him, and so she must love him. Sam also feels superior to Marion; he is the competent one, she the helpless nitwit, and that makes him feel good. While he patronizes Marion a good deal and tells her it's time she grew up, Sam would feel extremely insecure if she ever did, because then she might not need him any more.

But it could happen one day, if Sam were to lose his job or become ill, for instance. Childlike partners faced with this sort of crisis are sometimes forced to change roles—a situation that such a couple finds highly stressful. If Sam had to surrender his parenthood he might well feel threatened, degraded, or burdensome.

Another kind of father-partner, similar to Ibsen's Torvald, *forces* a wife who is not really childlike to be that way. The other side of that coin, of course, is a parental woman who treats her mate like a fool—the familiar bungling, impractical dolt of simple-minded television comedy.

Children often upset the equilibrium of a parental-childlike combination because, as the real children grow up, the childlike partner may identify closely and struggle to grow up with them.

Some parental partners accept such changes with reluctance but good grace, knowing in their hearts that they cannot prevent growth. Some may change themselves, and be relieved to give up the parental role. But others, who try to hold on to it, fight a series of last-ditch skirmishes in an effort to halt progress; they often destroy the partnership in the process.

Parental-Parental

Stormy. A Thurber-cartoonlike war of the sexes, a never-ending struggle for domination.

CHILDLIKE-PARTNER COMBINATIONS

Childlike-Childlike

These combinations are made up of two adults who go through life like children at play. Their world has no tomorrows and no one ever has to be responsible. It's fun to play, and they both have a good, good time until there is a crisis. Then—panic. Each wants a parent. But neither can rise to the occasion and become an adult. They are both disappointed and frustrated, and so they do what disappointed, frustrated children usually do—accuse, complain, and quarrel.

Some of these couples are just mature enough to take turns occasionally at playing a parental role. When this is the case, they can lead a good life. Otherwise, these partners can only hide in the sandbox of their relationship to protect themselves against the rest of the world. Some go through life like brother and sister playing house, indulging in incest without guilt.

RATIONAL-PARTNER COMBINATIONS

Rational-Parental

May do well, especially if Parent can play the rescuer role. Rational does not need to be rescued from drugs, alcohol, or the like, but rather from a lonely, dull, joyless life. Parental rescuer offers emotion and social vitality; rational pays back with order, certitude, dependability, love—even financial stability.

Rational-Other

Rationals get along with companionate and parallel partners—or almost anyone—as long as no one threatens their self-esteem. They are especially vulnerable because although they love and care, they find it difficult to be in touch with their feelings. For this reason they cannot tolerate demands for closeness.

COMPANIONATE-PARTNER COMBINATIONS

Companionate-Companionate

This is the common and the best possible combination for a companionate person. Neither partner expects love and they *are* good companions; they respect and take care of each other, and are unfailingly kind and considerate. Only an unexpected outside force (such as illness) or a major change in behavior on the part of one member is likely to shake such a couple.

Since companionate partners are willing to do without romance or passion (although they do want warmth and some closeness), this is not a common partnership among the young. One of its hazards comes from the tendency these mostly middle-aged (or older) couples have of living in the past rather than for the present or future. They are often in heated competition over who had a better life before, or, say, whose children are superior and give them more love and attention.

PARALLEL-PARTNER COMBINATIONS

Parallel-Parallel

Usually works well, and is the best combination for a parallel partner. As long as both partners remain parallel, and are compatible in other areas, they can have a good, comfortable relationship.

Parallel-Rational

This usually works well, too, as long as both feel easy about the compromises they must make. The major trouble area would be a demand from either (more likely the rational one) calling for the other to express more emotion—a task the parallel partner cannot fulfill.

Parallel-Companionate

Similar to the above. Partners get along unless Companionate begins to need more closeness.

Parallel-Parental or Parallel-Childlike

Destined to clash. If there is one thing Parallels do not want, it is being maneuvered into being anything other than themselves. They do not want to be children and they do not want to be parents; they *must* be accepted as they are.

In a typical interaction, Child, unable to push Parallel into becoming a Parent, may develop psychosomatic symptoms, throw temper tantrums, become critical and mean. At which point Parallel, pushed beyond endurance, will look for a safer relationship that is less demanding—or may, alternatively, even become severely disturbed.

Parallel-Other

It is not uncommon for all sorts of people to marry parallel partners in the mistaken belief that once they are married, they will grow ever closer together. It's not just a hope, but a challenge. If only they can give enough love, Parallel is bound to respond and give in return.

But Parallel, finally realizing what is expected, is filled with intense anguish. The only possible way to deal with such agony is to grow even more aloof; enough distance from the source is sure to kill the pain. It usually kills the marriage, too.

But there are some parallel partners who are less extreme and may actually be drawn a bit—but only a bit—closer. They frequently find themselves in situations like this one:

Marcia, a moderate parallel, is living with Pete, who, if he had to describe himself, would say that he was a nice old-fashioned romantic, the kind of guy who wants a warm, loving woman to be his intimate partner for life. But Pete's problem (a problem as common as crabgrass) is that he is mistaken about himself. Pete has all the trappings of a romantic, but the truth is he isn't really very comfortable in an intimate relationship. He has a variety of excuses for having broken off in the past with other women who were warm and loving; he attributes any number of flaws to their characters, but has never recognized that it was simply his need to flee from their warmth that made the affairs fail. Although he doesn't know it, Pete, in spite of his sentimentality, is not a romantic at all but a *pseudo*romantic and a borderline parallel partner.

When Pete met Marcia she seemed like the answer to his dreams. "She isn't anything like the others," he told his best friend, "not one of those who tells you all her troubles and her whole life story the minute you meet. Actually, she's almost a little bit formal—kind of stand-offish, reserved. I can't wait to break down her reserve and get her to like me as much as I like her."

So Pete set out to win the unwinnable prize, to break through Marcia's aloofness and make her love him. He made himself indispensable to her, catered to her every whim. When she wanted to swim, he rented a car and drove for three hours on a crowded highway to take her to her favorite beach. When she wanted to hike, he slogged around in the country for an entire rainy Sunday, happy to be by her side. He spent his salary, and borrowed more, to take her to the best restaurants and to shower her with small but carefully chosen "meaningful" gifts. Each time Marcia moved closer to him, Pete felt that he was proving again what a valuable and sexual person he was. And then she agreed to live with him.

As soon as they began life on a day-in-day-out basis, Pete's infatuation seemed to cool. He didn't make love to Marcia for a whole week—but, to his consternation, she didn't seem to notice. At once his ardor flared and he began to woo her again. Then, after another week or two, it was Marcia who grew cool, and Pete began to suffer acutely.

They have been going on that way for months now, push-pull, up-down. It is as if they're on an emotional seesaw; even though they don't like it, neither knows how to get off.

Pete and Marcia have a classic sadomasochistic relationship, but elements of this kind of interaction may appear in almost any kind of partnership combination. It is not culture-bound, either; there is a Caribbean maxim that says "No have: want, want. Have: no want, no want." Marcia gives Pete just enough "love" to keep him locked into their destructive relationship, and although he suffers because she never gives it when he wants it, she never puts him out of his misery by firmly ending the relationship. Pete is the one who gets the worse of it because he cares more. Marcia is not involved enough to be terribly vulnerable, so it is easier for her. But every time Pete sees how detached she can be, he needs to win her all over again.

There are other kinds of couples who interact in similar but much milder ways. They often perform ceremonial come-close–go-away dances, but these take place within mature relationships. With enough security, a little gentle and mutually agreed-to sadomasochistic play can bring a bit of extra spice to any couple's life.

Such subtleties and complexities furnish the excitement, the passion, the anguish or the joy of all intimate relationships. If two partners genuinely love each other, and if they have enough understanding of what they do and why they do it, they can redirect life together when it needs to be redirected. And if their mutual life is so good as to need no new directions, they can enhance and perpetuate the happiness and joy they have been sharing.

4

The Private Covenant

In the opening pages of this book we introduced several couples who were puzzled by their own behavior. To a greater or lesser degree, at least one member of each couple was doing something potentially damaging to the relationship—either without being aware of it or without knowing why. Pressed for an explanation, each could very likely have thought of one; when we have to we can all find reasons for what we do—but the reasons aren't necessarily true, and often they are so unconvincing that we don't even succeed in fooling ourselves with them.

Let's look again at Lucille and Bill Williams. (Lucille was the one who had just come home with a new dress she was sure Bill would like, but insead of really applauding the purchase, Bill had sounded irritated—then one word led to another and the Williams were embroiled in still another quarrel.) It's too bad that they get along so poorly now, because they used to be a very happy couple. They married a year after Bill finished law school. He was working at his first legal job and Lucille worked as a technician in a medical laboratory. With their combined salaries they were able to afford a two-bedroom apartment; Bill used the second bedroom as a study although it was understood that, eventually, it would become a nursery.

But Lucille was in no hurry for a baby. The oldest child of a large family, she had helped take care of the younger ones from the time she started school; Lucille still felt as if she had had enough babytending to last her for at least another few years. Bill, on the other hand, was an only child, conceived just about the time his parents had given up hope; when he was born, his father was forty-five years old. Bill was a lonely child who always thought of his father as an old man. He was extremely jealous of his friends who had sisters and brothers, and whose fathers took them on camping trips, taught them to ski, and were agile on the tennis court. Bill was determined not to cheat his own son by depriving him of siblings or by saddling him with an old-man father. Bill meant to have his family while he was still young enough to *do* things with them. He wanted, more than anything, to be a pal to his sons.

Bill said nothing to Lucille of these feelings—he wasn't even fully aware of some of them—but it wasn't long before he began gently to suggest that they have a child. At first, Lucille was able to make light of the matter and brush it aside. But as Bill became more insistent, she realized that this was important to him and so she gave in; she loved Bill a great deal and was eager to make him happy.

Lucille became pregnant almost immediately; although she was able to work right up to the time the baby was due, they didn't have a chance to save up as much money as they had planned. Lucille was disappointed that she couldn't furnish the nursery as lavishly as she had meant to, but she was busy and content during the last weeks of her pregnancy as she refinished the crib and chest she had bought at a yard sale.

The baby turned out to be a girl—and although Bill never said a word, he was dismayed; he had been absolutely certain he would have a son. A year later, he suggested they try again.

Lucille pointed out that they were chronically low on funds and that the apartment was too small for a family of four. Perhaps if they could just wait until she had a chance to get back to work for a couple of years. . . . But Bill wouldn't hear of it. He was afraid he would be an old father by the time he had a son. He said he would start to look around for a better-paying job right away.

It is seven years later. Bill got the job and he got a son. The Williams have bought a house in a good suburb, they own two cars, and they belong to the country club. They look like the ideal American family, but they aren't; they aren't nearly as happy as they were in the early days. In fact, they really aren't happy at all, but that's a hard fact for them to face, so they haven't ever talked about it. Each hopes that if they just wait a while, life will straighten out and everything will be all right again.

But it won't. It's been getting steadily worse and it will get worse still. Finally, Lucille and Bill will have to admit that their marriage is in serious trouble, and then, frightened, because they don't want to separate, they will probably decide to see a marital therapist. If the therapist is a good one, they might begin to understand what is wrong. And then, if they work hard enough, and in the right way, they might be able to fix it.

But it's too bad that they will have to go through all that—or even that they've gotten where they are—because they could have been spared a good bit of time, money, and suffering if they had known right away that each was furious with the other for not living up to the terms of *an agreement they never made,* an agreement we'll call a covenant. This isn't the usual marriage contract, or a business agreement, or any other kind of document either of them ever heard of. It isn't even a document. It exists only in their own minds—and there are two separate covenants, Lucille's and Bill's. Lucille *thinks* Bill has agreed to behave in a certain way if she behaves in a certain way. When he doesn't do what she expects, she feels angry. Bill, too, expects Lucille to live up to *his* imaginary covenant and is angry whenever she fails.

Are the Williams crazy, living in some kind of fantasy world? Not a bit of it. They are perfectly normal; almost every couple, everywhere, has separate covenants—and, like the Williams, they don't even know they exist.

Sociologist Jessie Bernard describes her concept of *his marriage* and *her marriage* in her book *The Future of Marriage*. She writes that when couples are questioned about such matters as how often they have sexual relations, what they talk about and how much, or which one makes the decisions, husbands and wives give such different answers that the two seem to be reporting on different marriages. "As I think they are," says Dr. Bernard. She points out that spouses perceive "facts" and situations differently according to their own needs, values, attitudes, and beliefs.

The idea can be carried far beyond the differences in perception between men and women. We have already seen that each partner behaves with the other in accordance with his or her behavioral profile. While once upon a time we would have labeled certain profiles as distinctly masculine or feminine, we wouldn't do so today. We recognize that all of us, men and women alike, may or may not want power, closeness, or distance, and that we all may be either active or passive, and so on.

We also know that at some times we are in full charge of our behavior and that at others we act in ways that baffle us. We are baffled when we are trying, in spite of what we *think* we want to do, to satisfy our unconscious psychological and biological needs, our inner needs. We have seen that some combinations are so poor that those ill-matched couples would have been better off if they had never gotten together in the first place. Happily, most of the time, really poor fits don't try. The majority of couples do make combinations that are workable—if they know how to make them work. They can do that best if they understand their individual covenants—*his* and *hers*— and then create just one that is *theirs:* a *couple covenant.*

To illustrate the principle of *his* and *her* covenants, let's focus further on the Williams; they have private covenants that are, in their basic outlines, like most others. Each covenant includes what that partner expects to get *from* the relationship and what he or she is willing to give *to* it; but too often a partner assumes that by living up to, say, his obligations (what he gives) he will receive everything he wants (what he expects to get). Bill's covenant is no exception. He believes, only partly consciously, that if he answers certain of

Lucille's needs as he perceives them it is then understood between them that she, in turn, will fill his needs—which he has failed to express to her.

The problem, of course, is that little is clearly understood between them. Lucille, in fact, has only a vague idea of what Bill expects of her. Some of the basics are plain enough: she knows that he expects her to be sexually faithful, to run the house, and to be chiefly responsible for the children. He also expects her to dress and behave appropriately in public, to attend his bosses' dinner parties and, once a year, to entertain the bosses and their spouses in turn. But there is much more that Lucille has never thought about—and quite a bit that Bill has never thought about, either.

What *does* Bill expect of her? And what is he prepared to give in order to get it?

We already know some of Bill's expectations: that he would have children while he was still young, that he would have more than one child, and that he would have a son. We know something about Bill's inner needs too: He is active enough to have gotten the kind of job that would make it possible for him to have the family he wanted. He is independent enough that, even though he loves his family, he would have preferred to have Saturday to himself so that he could finish his work.

Bill knows those things about himself, too. But he doesn't know why he was annoyed when Lucille bought that dress even though the mystery isn't too hard to solve. Bill was angry—as he often is—because Lucille failed to live up to a clause in his private covenant. The sequence goes like this: Bill urged Lucille to have a child, which meant that she had to give up her job. Then he urged her to have a second child, and that meant they had to have more living space. So they bought a house that is heavily mortgaged, they are paying off loans on the two cars they need in the suburbs, and the dues at the country club are steep. Bill makes enough money to keep everything going, and he is hopeful that he will soon be making much more. But living as close to the financial edge as they do makes him intolerably anxious—and he feels that Lucille should be earning money, too, sharing the burden like the real partner she used to be, instead of just spending. Unreasonable? You might say so—but since the whole notion is beyond Bill's awareness, there is no reason it *should* be reasonable. If Bill *thought* about it, or even knew about it, he would see how unreasonable it is—but he doesn't. That's why he precipitates a quarrel whenever Lucille spends money. Each time, he feels disappointed all over again that she isn't helping to earn money so as to ease his anxiety.

Now let's see what Lucille's covenant is like. Her original expectation was that she would keep her job (which she loved) and put off having children for several years—or at least until she and Bill had saved up enough money to tide them over while he climbed the economic ladder. However, she sacrificed her own ambitions so Bill could have what he wanted: she gave up her work, had two children in rapid order, moved from the city to the suburbs. Now she expects that since she became a suburban housewife to please Bill, he will fulfill his part of the bargain and be an ideal suburban husband. She expects him to make enough money to support the lifestyle to which they have become accustomed—but she doesn't like him to work on Saturdays to do it. That much she knows. What she doesn't know is that she needs much more warmth and closeness than Bill is able to give her. On a conscious, rational level, she knows that he works on Saturday because he hopes to get an important promotion and to make more money. On an unconscious level, she is jealous of the time and energy he puts into his papers and wishes he would lavish that time and attention on her instead. When she can't get Bill, she unconsciously gets even by spending his money. It makes him angry— but at least when they fight, she has his full attention. He has disappointed her by not being as intimate and affectionate as *her* covenant calls for.

The Williams' disappointments with each other are typical; since every private covenant includes not only what the partner expects to give, but *what he or she expects to get in return,* everyone is disappointed when the expected—and often unstated—benefits fail to materialize.

Covenants deal with every aspect of a couple's life: relationships with friends, achievements, power, sex, leisure time, money, closeness, children, and so on. The terms, or clauses, include those that are spoken aloud and those that are withheld, those that the individual is aware of and those that are unconscious. The way any couple gets along together is a direct reflection of how well they live up to the terms of each other's covenants—even if they are unaware of covenants, and whether or not they know each other's terms.

You can see further how covenants work if you think about them on a personal level. You are doubtless aware of some of your own expectations and needs, and you are doubtless aware of some of your partner's—but have you ever considered that whenever you try to fulfill your partner's needs, it is because you expect that, in return, he or she will then take care of yours? (It is only a romantic myth that real love always gives without thought of return.) And think about your having a secret covenant in your head and expecting your partner (who may not know the first thing about it) to live up to it. Then turn it around. Your partner has a secret covenant, too, one you may know little about. But you are expected to live up to it, and every time you don't, your failure might be held against you. It hardly seems fair, does it?

Obviously, you and your partner could avoid a lot of pitfalls if you understood your own covenants—with your needs, expectations, and what you will give clearly formulated—and had at least some knowledge of each other's. This would enhance your self-knowledge and communication; it could expose the reasons for a major part of any unhappiness you may have, and explain much of your apparently irrational behavior, bickering, or bitterness. Partners who understand the ways in which they have disappointed each other no longer have to feel helpless, because they are better able to solve their problems effectively instead of being made more miserable by them. To understand does not mean that you have to fulfill any impossible expectations, or to be someone you are not or do not wish to be. Understanding *does* make it possible to discuss and clarify the true issues between you and your partner—and knowing the issues is a prerequisite to settling them.

YOUR OWN COVENANT

Your own private covenant contains clauses that cover just about every area of your feelings, needs, interests, and relationships. To help you know what they are, here are some sample checklists. They don't cover every possibility, but they do cover the major points for most people. Select the items that are important for you, and look into how you feel about them. Add any others that you think of.

This is simply an exercise in awareness; there is no need for you to write anything, unless you want to.

Category I   My Intellectual Expectations of My Relationship

I want—*or* I do not want: *Or,* This is important—*or* not important—to me:

1. A mate who will be loyal, loving, exclusive.
2. A constant support against the rest of the world.
3. Insurance against loneliness.
4. To be part of a twosome instead of a single.
5. A solution to the chaos of life.
6. A relationship that must last "until death do us part."
7. Sanctioned and readily available sex.
8. To create a family.
9. The inclusion in my new family of people other than my mate who require prime consideration too: for example, my children, parents, friends; mate's parents, friends.
10. To acquire a ready-made family (in-laws, stepchildren) not just a mate.
11. My own home-refuge from the world.
12. A respectable position and status in society.
13. The creation, with my partner, of an economic and/or a social unit.
14. To be an all-encompassing image that will inspire me and my mate to work, build, accumulate.
15. A respectable channel for my aggressive drives—everything I do will be for my family, too, not just for me.

Category II   Expectations that Arise from My Inner Needs

Psychological and biological needs exist deep within yourself, and it will probably be more difficult for you to be clear on these points than those in Category I. But even if you are unaware of your feelings about some of these things, you will find that as you think about them, answers will begin to emerge.

1. Independence-Dependence

How well can I take care of, and function for, myself?

Do I want my partner to complete my sense of self—or to start what I can't start alone?

Do I feel as if I can't survive without my partner?

Is my sense of worth dependent on my partner's attitude or feeling toward me?

Am I dependent on my partner to initiate plans?

Am I dependent on my partner to set our taste, pace, style?

2. Activity-Passivity

How much desire and ability do I have to take the action necessary to get what I want?

Can I be active in reality as well as in idea?

If I'm passive, am I hostile to an active partner? For example, will I exercise veto power without suggesting alternatives?

3. Closeness-Distance

Do I become increasingly anxious as I expose my feelings, thoughts, and actions—or get closer to—my partner?

Do I dare to expose any personality or intellectual limitations I think I may have, or "frailties" such as cultural gaps, poor taste, childish behavior and so on?

Do I dare to let my partner really know me?

Can I communicate openly enough to make known my needs, to solve problems? Am I aware enough to share my feelings and experiences?

When my partner says "Tell me what you're thinking," do I perceive it as an intrusive, controlling inquiry, or as an invitation to open, intimate, and candid dialogue? Do I feel apprehensive, freeze, or go blank? Or can I be honest with myself and my partner?

Do I avoid closeness? Defend myself against it by making jokes, "needing" to do something at just that moment, or the like?

How urgently do I need my own living space? How strongly do I resist if someone intrudes on it?

4. Power: Use and Abuse

Can I share power? Or do I want it all? Or do I usually abdicate or delegate it to my partner?

Can I use power without ambivalence and anxiety?

Am I so afraid of not having power that I must always be in control?

Or do I always renounce my desire for power and assume

that my partner's power will be used in my behalf—then feel hurt and angry if it isn't?

    5. Dominance-Submission

        Do I generally submit or dominate?

        Do I subscribe to the seesaw thesis: if one of us is up, the other must be down?

        Can we resolve matters without one or the other submitting or dominating?

    6. Fear of Loneliness or Abandonment

        To what degree is my love for my partner based on my fear of being alone?

        What do I expect my partner to do to keep me from being lonely or to alleviate my fear of desertion?

        If I have fears about loneliness and desertion, how do they affect my behavior in the relationship? Do I cling? Find excuses to tag along?

        Have I chosen a mate who is likely to stay with me—or have I selected someone who is bound to feed my fear?

    7. Need to Possess and Control

        Can I feel easy about my mate's having initiative and outside interests and activities, or do I have to possess and control him or her in order to feel secure?

    8. Level of Anxiety

For physiological and psychological reasons, some people are more anxious than others, and anxious people often show their anxiety openly and directly. Others handle or try to prevent anxiety by using defense mechanisms against it. The resulting behavior often has great impact on the partner. Some common defense mechanisms have worked their way into our everyday language, for example: "He is *projecting* his own fears onto others," or "Don't *displace* your anger onto the dog when it's me you're sore at," or "Look at the facts and stop *denying* to yourself that we're heading for financial trouble."

        How do I behave when I am anxious?

        How do I behave when I am emotionally upset in other ways?

        How does my style of dealing with anxiety affect my partner?

    9. Response to Anxiety

        If my partner is anxious, how does that affect me?

        Can I accept it without feeling that I am to blame for it?

        Do I respond in such a way as to increase or decrease my partner's anxiety?

    10. Gender Identity

        How secure do I feel about my own maleness or femaleness?

Do I depend on my partner to make me feel like a man or a woman?

Am I defensive or aggressive in affirming my manhood or womanhood?

11. Characteristics Wanted in Sex Partner

In order to enjoy sex, what do I ask of a partner?

What personality traits, physical characteristics, graces, and role assumptions do I like?

Are such attributes as achievement, the ability to handle emergencies, be a protector, survive easily, and the like important to me in a partner?

12. Acceptance of Self and Others

Can I love myself as well as my partner?

Am I so self-involved that I can't love anyone else?

Does love make me feel so vulnerable that I have to avoid it in order to feel safe?

13. Cognitive Style

Partners often approach issues or perceive entire situations differently. Although they both see and hear the same things, they may select different data for consideration or may reach different conclusions concerning the same data. For example, when Norma and Dirk went shopping for a house they went about it in completely different ways: Norma inspected basements for leaks, the sizes of hot water tanks, the kinds of heating equipment, the thickness of beams, and so forth. Upstairs she checked windows, plumbing, closets, and mentally tore down walls to turn two small rooms into one large one. Dirk, on the other hand, was inclined to make snap judgments; he liked the imposing position of a house on top of a knoll, was charmed by the fake-plantation-house pillars on another, rejected several because they "just don't look like the place I want to live in." Houses either appealed to him or not; the reasons he gave were based on first impressions and were highly subjective. Norma, on the other hand, was not ready to say what she thought about any house until she had inspected it thoroughly and considered its pros and cons. Arguments rarely resolve such differences between a pair; often neither accepts the fact that they have to work with two sets of perceptions, and neither has much respect for the other's style. This is a common source of conflict. While we are all accustomed to approving with, *"Vive la différence!"* when we refer to dissimilarities in gonads, we are unfortunately unable to celebrate similarly the contrasts in cognitive style. This is an area that is frequently overlooked, even by marital therapists, although it deserves major attention. For example, with Norma and Dirk, it would be useful to consider Norma's objective criteria along with Dirk's more subjective, less defined, but very definite esthetic judgments. If Dirk liked a house, Norma would then check it out for practical value. If she felt a house was an especially good buy because of its excellent condition, Dirk could then assess it according to his criteria of location, design, and his own emotional reactions. Between them they could do what neither could do alone.

> To find out about your own cognitive style, ask yourself:
>
> Am I very different from my mate in style? In intelligence (which may but does not necessarily affect style)?
>
> Do I respect my partner's style?
>
> Does my partner respect mine?
>
> Do I feel inferior?
>
> Do I feel superior?
>
> Am I dissatisfied because of differences in cognitive styles between us?
>
> Can we complement one another by supplying different but important viewpoints regarding our joint decisions?

Now that you have read over the "want lists," you have a basis for asking yourself what you really expect and/or need from your relationship. Give yourself some time to think about it, and then try this: What do you think of as your contributions to the relationship? Assuming that your mate has a "want list" of his or her own, how much of it are you familiar with? What do you do about filling his or her needs? Do you decide on your own what you will give (whether it is wanted or not) or do you ask your partner, and talk it over together? And most important of all: Have you considered that you do what you do for your partner in order to get what you want for yourself? Has it ever occurred to you that you could make trades? "I know it worries you if I leave the office late and forget to call you—so I *will* call, I promise. But if I do, will you get up and have breakfast with me on weekends? I feel so alone when you don't; it gets me off to a bad start for the whole day." We'll return to the matter of quid pro quos a little later. First, the last part of the private covenant.

Category III   Apparently External Problem Areas

Many couples point to outside factors as causes of their disharmony. They are usually in error, however, which is why the word *apparently* appears above. Problems that seem to stem from external sources most often come from the disappointments indicated in Categories I and II. The kinds of problems cited in this part are usually the ones couples become aware of first. If you face any of them you will probably, on the basis of what has gone before, recognize that some of your problems actually come from inner clashes you might not have identified before.

Unlike the first two lists, the items in this one apply not just to you, but to the way you and your partner interact as a couple.

1. Communication

How open are we, and how clear, in the way we give and receive key information? (Couples often say "Our communication broke down"—as if it were a piece of machinery, independent of them.)

Can we easily and honestly express love, understanding, anxiety, anger, our wants, and our fears? Or are we afraid of revealing shortcomings or not living up to what we believe is our partner's idealized image of us?

2. Lifestyle

Are our lifestyles alike enough so that we are, in the main, compatible?

Or are they so different that we can choose only between strife or subjugation? Can we accept liking some of the same things but not agreeing on others?

Do we go our different ways, leading parallel lives?

Is one of us a "day person" and the other a "night person"?

Is one gregarious, the other a loner?

Is one an indoor, the other an outdoor person?

Does one prefer meat and potatoes, the other gourmet cooking?

Do we have other basic differences in taste—in leisure activities, friends, dress, decor, preference for family *versus* friends, and so on?

Do these reflect differences that are even more basic?

3. Families

Does either of us resent the other's family or the way he or she relates to them? Or any individual members of that family—mother, father, sibling?

Do we have divided loyalties?

How do we, as a couple, handle family visits?

How successfully do we make decisions concerning our relationships with our individual families?

Is either of us overly childlike in these dealings? Or overly parental?

4. Child Rearing

Who has more authority with the children?

How do we make decisions about bringing up our children and taking care of them?

Do we compete for their love?

Is one of us more permissive than the other?

5. Relationships with Children

What alliances are made with the children? Is one "Mommy's girl"? Or "Daddy's"? Why? Do the alliances serve any purposes I (we) haven't thought about before?

If we have children from previous marriages, how do they affect our relationship?

6. Family Myths

Do we join in maintaining family myths? Do we go out of our way to present to others a particular image of our relationship, our family, ourselves (that we are wealthy, intellectual, of a high social class, very loving, and so on)?

7. Money

Who makes how much?

Who spends it?

Who is in charge of the funds?

Who does the bookkeeping?

Do I (we) view money as power?

Do we view money as love?

8. Sex

Do we both regard sex as pleasure, or solely for having children? Do we approach it with a lack of enthusiasm or as a duty to the other?

Do we have different attitudes about how often we should have sex?

Who initiates it?

Do we differ about approaches to sex (homosexual, heterosexual, bisexual, fetishistic, or group), ways to achieve or heighten gratification (drugs, playing out of fantasy), fidelity?

How do my (our) feelings of love and consideration interrelate with sex and its fulfillment?

9. Values

Are we in general agreement on such priorities as money, culture, schools, home, clothes, personal moral codes, religion, politics, other relationships?

10. Friends

What attitudes do we have toward each other's friends?

What does each of us want from friends?

Can we share friends and each have our own as well?

What ground rules do we have about socializing with friends at work, personal friends, opposite-sex friends?

Do we both understand that we can't (and shouldn't try) to fulfill all of each other's emotional and recreational needs?

11. Roles

What responsibilities do we expect each to assume?

Who does the housework, cooking, shopping?

Who takes the major responsibility for earning the income, for child care, vacation and leisure-time plans, entertainment, financial planning?

Do we assign tasks along traditional gender lines or can we share them and be flexible enough to suit our needs at any given time? Do we consider each other's priorities and preferences?

How do we arrive at decisions about the above—jointly, by decree, or by just quietly going ahead with what each thinks is best?

12. Interests

Does either of us, when interested in a particular activity, insist that the other share it? Do we feel anxious, guilty, or at odds if we don't always join forces?

Do we respect, or resent, differences in work- or leisure-related interests?

Which interests are expressions of individuality, which are expressions of a need for distance? Or, conversely, for clinging and dependence?

With so many possibilities for disparity, it is evident that when two partners have two different covenants, they can easily run into trouble. Another, and somewhat more subtle, source of difficulty is conflict within *one* partner's own private covenant. It is not unusual for anyone to have conflicting needs that confuse the terms of his or her covenant. Edna Gordon was a woman in this predicament when she and her husband, Paul, sought professional help.

Edna is a contemporary woman, and her problems are representative ones. She was raised in a small town in a conservative section of the country and trained from birth to be "feminine"; she grew up *knowing* that her role in life was to be a wife and mother.

But by the time Edna married and had children, she had been exposed to a great many new influences, and she began to want very much to use her fine mind and her college education to pursue a career. At the same time, she had an overpowering need to be taken care of by a strong, effective, parental man—an apt description of the man she married.

At this point, Edna had a serious conflict. She was ambitious enough, and competent enough, to want a full-time outside career. But by the terms of her own covenant, she expected the love and protection of her parental husband; in exchange, she had been gladly willing to give her time and energy to care for their children and home. Now, the terms of her covenant no longer suited her primary need, so Edna switched the deal.

She took a full-time job on the assumption that Paul would cut down his own work hours to help out with the children after the baby-sitter left each day. Paul had never agreed to any such thing (and Edna had never even discussed it with him)—but Edna had revised her covenant so that she now took his help with the kids for granted. When Paul refused to do what she expected, Edna felt betrayed. In furious outbursts, she accused him of trying to keep her tied down so that she couldn't achieve anything on her own.

So Paul, in an effort to go along with Edna, did make some time to help take care of the children. But to his surprise, whenever he did, instead of feeling happy about it, Edna became anxious. Even though she had revised her covenant so that she could fulfill her need for an independent career, she still felt so committed to her original covenant that she felt guilty because she wasn't a "proper" mother. It seemed obvious to her that if she didn't live up to her original obligations, Paul wouldn't live up to his: he would stop loving her.

Edna's conflicts were so severe that her family's life was completely disrupted, and it was Paul who finally insisted that the couple seek professional help.

Early in the course of treatment Edna and Paul became familiar with the principle of covenants. To find out what their own were, they were urged to consider their *awareness* of covenant terms on three different levels. You can do the same thing.

Level I.   Conscious: Verbalized

This includes what you actually tell your partner about your expectations in clearly understood language. For instance, "I've been concerned about my father since his heart attack and I'd like to visit him regularly once a week now, so that he has something he can look forward to and count on. It will make me feel better about him." This is a *direct message,* very different from "It would be nice if we could visit my father more often now" or "Let's try to look in on my father a little more." Wants and loosely defined plans are sometimes plainly heard by one's mate, but frequently they are not. Even a seemingly clear communication can be shut out if the listener has a different idea in mind. No matter how distinct the broadcast, no accurate communication takes place until the message has been fully received.

Level II.   Conscious but Not Verbalized

This refers to those expectations, plans, beliefs, fears, and fantasies that you have and *know* you have but choose not to discuss with your partner. You may be ashamed to disclose certain things, wary that a revelation will incur your mate's anger or make him or her think less of you. Your uncertainties about entering a fuller relationship, entering potential areas of disagreement, and revealing disappointments are illustrative of the kinds of things one often considers but hesitates to mention. Partners rarely conspire to keep silent; if we hide our thoughts and feelings from the people we love, it is usually because of fear.

Level III.   Beyond Awareness

These are the desires and needs that you have but don't *know* you have. They are often unrealistic and contradictory, as Edna's were. Most often they are inner needs, particularly those involving power and control, closeness and distance, active-passive impulses, child-adult or gender-identity conflicts, and the like. In many respects, this is a very significant covenant level because it produces so many subtle yet crucial modes of behaving and relating.

While you are ordinarily unaware of this level in yourself, you can often discover it in part if you look hard. One way is to reflect on the thoughts that make you uneasy so that you push them away. Your mate may actually be somewhat more aware of your unconscious needs than you are. Later, when we discuss how couples can use their individual covenants to forge one covenant between them, you will note that you and your partner can often shed light on each other's unconscious as well as contradictory terms. Women will frequently say "I know he likes to act strong and possessive—but I also realize how dependent he is on me, how like a little boy he is in many ways." And men often say "She's in constant conflict. She really wants to be independent and to go her own way—and at the same time, she wants me to be Big Daddy and take care of her." It is natural for men and women to have mixed feelings; virtually everyone has them about some things or at some times.

THE PRIVATE COVENANT: A SUMMARY

Now that we have covered the elements of the private covenant, let's sum up:

The term *private covenant* refers to the total set of each partner's expressed and unexpressed, conscious and unconscious ideas about (1) his or her responsibilities within the couple relationship and (2) the benefits he or she expects to get from the relationship in general and from the partner in particular.

The terms of private covenants are determined by the deep needs and wishes that partners expect their relationships to fulfill for them. They may include healthy and realistic needs as well as needs that are so unrealistic or conflicting that it is impossible for anyone to satisfy them.

The most important aspect of all is the *reciprocal nature* of the covenants: Partners expect that, because they give, they will receive in exchange.

While most people are, to some extent, aware of their own needs and wishes, they do *not* usually realize that their attempts to satisfy their partners' needs are based on the assumption that the partner will then reciprocate.

Furthermore, partners are only remotely—if at all—aware of their mates' expectations. They often assume that there is mutual agreement on a covenant when, in fact, there is none whatsoever. They act, however, as if an actual contract existed and both partners were committed to live up to its terms. When either one fails—and it is inevitable that each should fail from time to time—the disappointed partner reacts with rage, injury, depression, or withdrawal; the reaction is exactly the same as if a written agreement had been broken. This reaches its worst point when the aggrieved one feels that he or she has lived up to every obligation and then been let down—betrayed—by a seemingly uncaring, treacherous, or defaulting mate.

5
Rules of the Game

If it's true that each member of a
couple has a private covenant, how, you may well ask, do any couples ever manage to get along with each other at all?

It is a good question and it has a good answer. When any two people play a game together—tennis, gin, chess, Ping-Pong—they have private covenants and yet they get along. Each player has individual expectations of the game—recreation, distraction, companionship, the excitement of competing, exercise of mind or body—and most of the time, both players have one expectation in common: each hopes to win. The players also have certain obligations; the chief one is to provide the other person with a reasonable amount of pleasure so that he or she will continue to play. The limitation on that is that each one will usually try as hard as possible to win. (The only principle that distinguishes a game from a war is that one doesn't try to win at any cost.) The responsibility of keeping one's opponent sufficiently involved is as important as trying to win, and so one observes the rules of the game. The player who breaks them— who cheats, lies, hurls abuse, insults, or tennis racquets—soon has no one to play with. But as long as both players observe the rules they can compete and, at the same time, be friendly and have a good time. They get along.

And so it is with couples. Even though they have some private goals as well as joint ones, if they play the game according to the rules, they get along—to one degree or another. It's harder than in tennis, though, because the rules aren't posted in the clubhouse. Each couple has to make its own rules and, even then, the rules are never hard and fast but can be changed at will. In fact, since life is a far more complex game than tennis or gin, the rules *have* to be changed constantly to fit constantly changing situations.

A major life change comes when two people join forces emotionally and physically to become a couple. At this point they cease to be merely two individuals but are, in addition, a new social unit, a partnership. Like a business or any other kind of partnership, the whole is different from its component parts; it isn't only the sum of two personalities with their individual hopes and needs, but a new entity with hopes, needs, and responsibilities all its own. If John and Mary, good friends and tennis partners, married, they might not be aware of the separate character of the marriage. If, however, they went into business together, they would recognize instantly that the business was an entity apart from the two of them. The needs of the business— a restaurant, say—would include a building, a cook, kitchen equipment, tables, chairs, and patrons. And the new partners might find out that while they are both nice people in general, John is a terrible cook but a good waiter, and Mary is a poor bookkeeper but an excellent chef, bartender, what-have-you.

In married life, partners function in various ways, too, within their couple system and outside it in many other systems. We all say such things as "She's a great mother and a fine musician, but she's certainly no friend to her husband." Or "He's a considerate, loving friend and a magnificent gardener, but he can't seem to hold a job." Without thinking in technical terms, we often define people according to the way they function in different systems or the different roles they play.

Like a restaurant business, a couple system becomes a "third party" with a life of its own. And like a prosperous restaurant, it may help the partners get what they want; or, like a failing restaurant, it may make them miserable. A partnership can also affect either or both partners enough *to change the way they function in other systems.* The restaurant, for example, might keep John from being as good a father as he would like to be, because of its demanding hours. Mary, on the other hand, might now function better at home, since cooking in the restaurant may have sharpened her skills and taught her some new tricks.

It was in much the same fashion that marriage changed Bill Williams, the young attorney we met earlier. Although Bill started out as a rather noncompetitive person, when he was pressured to earn more money so that he could have the family he wanted and support it in middle-class suburban style, he became highly competitive. And Lucille changed, too. When Bill urged her to give up her job and raise a family, she began to envision different goals for herself and their couple system. Formerly indifferent to wealth and what it could buy, Lucille now feels that she *needs* the country club, two cars, and the good clothes that are the cornerstones of her way of life.

Couples, married or not, find that their desires, needs, and functions constantly change, and as they do, those changes in turn change the partnership. It is altered the moment one gives up his or her home and moves in with the other, and yet again as soon as the two decide on a new financial arrangement; it shifts each time they decide who will do what kind of work, whenever they decide where to go, whom to see, whether or not to move, take a vacation, buy a car, even go to the movies. Each partner is always, to some extent, at the mercy of the partnership. When a partnership breaks down the angry partners think, in effect, "Surely *I* didn't have anything to do with the creation of this monster [the system]; it doesn't even come close to my expectations [covenant]."

And it's true that a partnership, even for those who *are* getting along well, may be very different from what one might expect the partners' individual covenants to produce. This is so because it is within the system that the two partners are maneuvering to fulfill the terms of their own private covenants. That is what gives a couple system the elements of a game, a game each player is trying to win even while they both observe certain rules. They are operating according to a set code of behavior; they engage in all kinds of strategies they have developed in their many dealings with each other. Some of the rules of their game are good for the couple, some are bad. And all of them are subject to change every time the individuals and their interactions change. Some of the rules are known to both, some are not—an important difference from a game.

Like two tennis players who will stop playing with each other unless they enjoy it, the couple, to remain a couple, must collaborate to gratify their major needs and wishes. And they have to do so without becoming so aggressive or so anxious that they destroy the system—the game. They must satisfy *its* major needs at the same time that they are trying to satisfy their own.

Clearly, all partners are constantly involved in a challenge— especially when you consider that virtually all individual covenants contain some clauses that are unrealistic and ambivalent. Both partners are trying to win satisfaction for their basic wishes and desires, realistic or not, and every time either partner makes a gain, the other one sets up an elaborate system of defensive maneuvers.

ASSERTIVE AND DEFENSIVE COUPLE PATTERNS

At any given moment, then, most partners are trying to fulfill their own needs, strengthening their defenses against the other's threat to the system's balance, and trying to do what they think best for the partnership. Like professional athletes, each is trying to win, each is being as defensive and offensive as possible, but at the same time they want to make the game (the system) a good one—and they want it to continue.

In couple relationships as in sports matches, winning moves are *assertive* ones. Assertiveness involves independence, activity, initiative, the use of authority or control, and a willingness to postpone immediate satisfaction to achieve a more distant goal. The various goals that partners want to achieve, however, are not always as clearcut as the goals of athletes: people may be adult and realistic in their interpersonal relationships, but they may also be infantile and unrealistic or neurotic; their goals and assertions may help the relationship or harm it. They may act consciously or unconsciously. In sum, assertive moves may be either positive or negative.

Defensive maneuvers also vary. Partners may act defensively to protect their own assertive moves, or to protect themselves against the other's assertive moves. They also need to defend their partnership as it moves to reach its goals, and to defend it and themselves against threats from the outside. Anything that disturbs their balance of force is likely to produce a defensive maneuver designed to re-establish it. Partners can be united in their defense maneuvers or, when they are at cross-purposes, they can use defenses against each other. In the last instance, new assertion-defense patterns are set in motion as the couple tries to resolve its differences. The net result may be either good or bad for the partnership. However, the way the two partners assert and defend, together and separately—the sum total of their feelings and acts as they play the game according to their own rules—*is* the couple's relationship.

Gregory, a sales manager for a large corporation, has had a poor year: his department showed a small drop in sales while all the other sections did better this year than last. Gregory is worried that he might lose his job; worse, he is worried about himself. He keeps thinking that there is something wrong with him. Is he less bright than the other sales managers? Less able to deal with his staff? Lacking in imagination, drive, competence? It occurs to Gregory that he's less of a person than he thought he was. And probably less than his boss thought he was. But his boss hasn't said anything to him, or treated him any differently, so maybe he hasn't noticed yet. Or maybe he has and is waiting for the right moment to confront Gregory with his inadequacies. Gregory mulls over the possibilities endlessly.

And his anxiety doesn't end with the work day; Gregory, like all of us, carries over feelings from one role or system to another. He has begun to feel like a fraud at work, afraid his boss will "find him out"; unconsciously, he expects Eleanor, his wife, to find him out, too. Although he doesn't know it, Gregory has become intensely anxious over the possibility of Eleanor's leaving him because he isn't good enough for her any more.

As his anxiety grows, Gregory sets up an elaborate defense system against it. Afraid that Eleanor will reject him, he counteracts by finding fault with her and by pushing her away from him. Almost everything Eleanor does annoys him. He can't stand her girlish giggle, her habit of dabbing at her nose with a tissue; he is infuriated by her daily telephone conversations with her sister, the way she messes up the newspaper, and her habit of losing her glasses. Worse, he grows increasingly upset over her insensitivity to his plight at work. He makes no allowance for the fact that he has never told her one thing about it.

After a time, Gregory has become angry enough with his wife that he doesn't care so much whether she leaves him or not. He has managed to relieve his anxiety over this to some degree and has, for the moment, lost sight of the fact that his marriage is far more important to him than anything else.

By this time, poor Eleanor is totally baffled. She doesn't know why Gregory is so cold, distant, and cross, and she can't get him to talk about it. She begins to think he doesn't love her any more, and is terribly threatened and upset. But, unlike him, she is aware of how important her marriage is, and she launches several maneuvers designed to be positively assertive, directed at keeping the marriage intact. Eleanor begins to cook Gregory's favorite dinners, she has her hair restyled, and is determined to remain cheerful, charming, and loving no matter what he says or does.

But the more loving she is, the more removed Gregory becomes. There doesn't seem to be any way Eleanor can get close to him, and she begins to wonder if there's someone else in his life, if he might be thinking of leaving her. Now *Eleanor* begins to make negative defensive moves: she becomes furious when Gregory walks in from the yard and tracks mud across the floor, complains when he doesn't shovel snow from the path before breakfast, screams when he leaves a few hairs in the bathroom sink.

Both Eleanor and Gregory suffered the same anxiety—that they would be abandoned—but neither was able to deal with it in a positive way. Although they defended themselves, they both acted in ways that were destructive to their couple system, marriage. If they had understood what was happening, they could have acted positively to strengthen a cardinal purpose of their marriage—that neither would ever be abandoned. It would have been relatively easy for them to reassure each other, relieve their anxieties, and make their marriage better instead of worse.

If Eleanor had known that Gregory feared losing his job, the two of them might have united against that outside threat instead of setting up individual defenses against each other. It might have been enough, early on, for Eleanor to reassure Gregory simply by reminding him that his department had excelled for several years running, that only a year before he had received a special award from his firm. Or it is possible that the two of them would have decided to withdraw their savings and start a small business of their own—something they had often talked of doing. Couples frequently act together in this way and become strongly assertive to defend themselves against a threat. And sometimes they do the opposite and become so completely demoralized that they don't do anything at all.

There are other possibilities. Some couples defend themselves by shifting their attention away from a problem altogether and focusing on something else that provides temporary distraction: "Let's have another baby." "Let's take a vacation." "Let's move." Still others act together to construct a defense that isn't appropriate to the threat at hand. This is a *folie à deux,* a maneuver based on commonly shared misperceptions. This is likely to isolate the couple from their friends but it does preserve the partnership since they can then feel "It's us against the world."

In a mild form of *folie à deux,* a couple can defend themselves against the flaws in their interaction by telling themselves "We are a loving couple who never fight" or acknowledge that they do have troubles but blame them on outside people or events: "If it hadn't been for your mother's interference it never could have happened," or "If only I had become pregnant . . . ," "If the market hadn't gone down when it did . . . ," "If I had gotten the job in Chicago. . . ."

Such defense mechanisms can be used by partners individually as well as together. Their importance can hardly be overstressed since they play such a key part in the way couples function. Although we have illustrated some destructive uses of defenses, they can often relieve stresses on a partnership and lead to the fulfillment of goals.

PLAYING GAMES

While we have used games as analogies to couple life, some couples *literally* play games with each other all the time. Not card or athletic games, but special games of their own invention. Although they are always to some degree unique, they tend to fall into categories that you will probably recognize.

Double Bind

Don and Eloise Washington have been married for four years. The marriage would be a pretty good one if Don's inner needs weren't in conflict. As things stand, he wants Eloise to share the power—but whenever she does he becomes fearful that she will boss him around. He is often angry and resentful; it seems to Eloise that no matter what she does, they wind up in a wrangle.

The latest one cropped up over getting the car inspected. Although Don had always handled this before, he had an unusually busy week ahead, so he said to Eloise, "Why is it always my job to take care of the car? You use it just as much as I do. Can't you run it down for the inspection?"

"Sure," Eloise said. "I'll be glad to. The only thing is that you said you thought the front wheels were out of alignment."

"So what?" Don answered. "If it needs work, it needs work. You can take care of it just as well as I can."

That night when Don came home the car was still at the service station and Eloise told him that she had authorized the seventy-two dollars worth of work the mechanic said was necessary for the car to pass inspection.

"Seventy-two bucks!" Don exploded. "You've got to be kidding! That guy must have seen you coming a mile away. How dumb can you be? I should have known better than to send you down there."

Eloise, who has been through this all too many times before, knows that there isn't much she can do. She is in the familiar, classic Double Bind: anything she does is wrong.

If she tries to argue with Don, he will become even angrier. If she doesn't argue, she knows she will withdraw and feel increasingly depressed. And she knows that Don can't tolerate her depression any more than an argument—if anything, it seems to make him even *more* angry. Predictably, this time is no exception. He begins to yell at Eloise; the sound of his loud, abusive voice breaks the spell of her muteness and she begins to yell back. They reach fever pitch, go on screaming for a couple of minutes more, then finally begin to simmer down. Eloise curls up in a corner with a book and Don goes to watch television. They don't say another word to each other for the rest of the night.

The Washingtons are double-bind-prone because Don has inner needs that are antagonistic: he wants his wife to share the power, yet he can't stand her having power because he is afraid she will win control and dominate him. Don communicates clearly enough when he urges Eloise to take responsibility, and she interprets the communication accurately—knowing that no matter what she does she is going to be in trouble. There is absolutely no way to please Don in this kind of transaction, nor any way Eloise can escape from the transaction or her husband's wrath. The only hope the Washingtons have is that Don will begin to understand his conflicting needs and the nature of his double-bind messages.

The Washingtons' game looks like a game without winners—but it has an important aspect that might be the payoff: the double-bind keeps the partners distant. While it has never occurred to them that this might be what they deliberately seek, every time Don's rage triggers Eloise's and the fighting escalates, it effectively diverts any closeness that might have been developing at the time that Don delivered his double-bind message.

You're Mother and Father to Me

It is not news that a woman frequently seeks her father in her partner and that a man often looks for his mother in his. Through the mechanism of transference, people expect their mates to exhibit a variety of real or fictitious attributes, ideals, or behavior that they ascribe to their opposite-sex parent.

What is far less well known is that men and women often transfer their feelings not only about one parent but about *both* parents onto a partner. As you might imagine, the amount of confusion and ambivalence that results rules out any possible satisfaction of needs. In addition to Double Bind, Don Washington played You're Mother and Father to Me with Eloise regularly. In fact, it is this game that gave rise to the other.

Don's mother had been a strong, controlling woman whom Don feared, and in order to avoid her disapproval he was almost always well-behaved and meek—just like his father. But Don despised his "gutless" father, who was always at his wife's mercy—and Don didn't want to despise Eloise. It seemed to him that he could only love her if she were powerful. But if she were to become really powerful, she would be like his mother, and then Don would have to become meek and submissive in order to get along with her. No wonder it was impossible for his wife ever to please him!

Don't Worry

When the famous psychiatrist William Alanson White defined maturity in his book, *The Interpersonal Theory of Psychiatry,* he noted that a mature person has "a very lively sensitivity to the needs of the other and to the interpersonal security or absence of anxiety in the other."

The way partners deal with each other's anxiety and their defenses against it is critical to the quality of the entire relationship. Insensitivity to a mate's insecurity, or the inability or unwillingness to assuage it, are everyday causes of couple strife and unhappiness.

Ideally, as soon as one partner senses that the other is anxious, he or she makes every effort to allay the anxiety—as this successful couple, Alex and Josie, do most of the time:

Alex is about to leave for Chicago on a business trip that will keep him away for several days. The last time he was in Chicago, some years ago, he ran into a former girlfriend in the hotel lobby. They had a few drinks together, talked over old times, had a few more drinks, and before the evening was out had gone to bed. Afterward Alex felt genuinely sorry about it; eventually he told Josie. She was upset but seemed to understand that it was a one-time event, and the matter was never discussed again.

Now, however, since Alex is returning to the scene of the crime, Josie feels uneasy. Even though she has told herself a dozen times that it is extremely unlikely, she is deeply worried that Alex might meet the same woman and do it again. Because she is feeling jittery, she picks a quarrel at the last minute—and now her anxiety really soars; if Alex goes away angry he probably *will* be unfaithful.

Alex, sensing her distress, doesn't leave, although it is nearly plane time. Instead, he takes a moment to put his arms around Josie; he tells her that he loves her, that he understands how she feels, and wants her to know she has nothing to worry about. By the time he walks out the door, Josie is feeling thoroughly reassured and the two part with loving feelings.

A few months later, Alex invites his elderly father to visit, and while he is there, the old man suffers a stroke. Alex calls an ambulance but it seems to take an eternity to arrive. He is, understandably, filled with anxiety, afraid his father might die, and Josie is almost as anxious as Alex. First, because she is very fond of the father, but second, because she has a morbid fear of illness and death. She is terrified by the sight of the stricken man lying on the living-room floor—and even more terrified that he will die before help arrives. But even under these circumstances, she thinks of Alex and what he must be feeling; she looks at the clock, assures him that only five minutes have passed, that the ambulance is bound to arrive within seconds, that her uncle had a stroke and made a good recovery, that the two of them will remain in the hospital overnight to see how things go, and so on. In spite of her own feelings, she makes every effort to comfort her partner. Josie and Alex have an excellent way of dealing with each other's anxiety—but not all couples do. This ability to be aware of and to relieve a partner's anxiety (without feeling responsible for it) helps any partnership. Unfortunately some partners are just as intuitive about escalating each other's negative feelings or letting their own anxiety be triggered by their mates.

I Didn't Know There Was Anything Wrong

Andy and Lorraine are a case in point. It is important to Andy that Lorraine see him as a strong person who can handle everything that comes along. However, he *cannot* handle everything; although he would never admit it, he needs Lorraine to be strong, and whenever she isn't, he becomes acutely anxious. It would destroy his self-image if she were ever to know that, so he has found a way around the dilemma. Whenever Lorraine needs Andy to be strong, he becomes totally deaf to her calls for help. Instead of responding with the sympathy and support she wants and needs, he thinks of some trivial thing to find fault with, becomes angry and impatient, and manages to start a fight. In this way, over the years he has managed to withdraw every time Lorraine needed him most. Consequently she has been consistently disappointed in her expectation that he would be there for her to lean on, and as a result, her love and respect for him are all but gone.

Andy has ruined his relationship by defending himself against exposure; it has never been his intention to hurt Lorraine or to fail her—in fact, he meant to do just the opposite—but his need to hide his weakness made him seem hostile and withdrawn.

Give Me

It is also common for two partners to have the same kind of basic insecurity, yet lack the ability to help each other combat it; instead, they repeatedly hurt each other and their partnership. The problem is not that they are mean but that they don't recognize each other's anxiety; all they can see are the defenses against it. Eleanor and Gregory were such a couple and the Hopkins are another.

Carol and Walter Hopkins both suffer from a deep fear of abandonment. Carol's defense is to seek constant reassurance—and for her, love means being taken care of materially. So Carol never stops wanting new things and comforts. She tells Walter pointedly about the fur coat she admired in a shop, the magnificent bracelet her friend got from her husband for Christmas; she *must* have a new color television set for the den, a tropical vacation, a membership at a health spa. The more anxious Carol becomes, the more goods and attention she craves as gifts from her husband. These, to her, are important evidence that he still loves her.

Walter, with the same inner anxiety as Carol's, doesn't find any comfort in material things at all, but in people. He needs to be surrounded by friends and many flattering, fawning, "yes" men and women. He tells himself that he must be worthy if so many people want to be with him.

Carol is as baffled by Walter's need for constant company as he is by her endless demands for things. Carol translates Walter's behavior as meaning that she doesn't satisfy his needs for love and friendship, although she is a loving person. She is deeply hurt, often jealous—and her fears of abandonment increase each year. So does her need for material reaffirmation.

Walter, for his part, can't understand why Carol is so exploitive. "No matter what you get, it's never enough," he complains. "If I buy you diamond earrings, you want a necklace to match. You get a new sofa, you need an Oriental rug to go with it. Do you think I'm made of money? Won't you ever stop?"

If only Carol and Walter understood each other's needs, they would both feel less threatened; instead of escalating their fears and their fights, they could be real partners and help each other.

You Fix Mine and I'll Fix Yours

Some partners have the thoroughly unrealistic hope that the other one will handle their anxiety and make it go away, or will provide an attribute that they lack. A socially shy woman with a deep fear of abandonment may select a gregarious man who also has a deep fear of abandonment. Because they are outwardly so different, each expects the other will "fix everything," and when they begin to recognize that this isn't possible, they feel deceived, cheated—and angry. If they understood that they both had the same anxieties, they could learn to support each other in ways that are genuinely, not superficially, complementary.

The Andersons: Their Covenants and the Rules of Their Game

Let us share now an actual case history; it provides a working model of all we have discussed so far—behavioral profiles, individual covenants, couples' games and couples' interactional scripts. Relate your own partnership to that of the Andersons as their therapy unfolds. (This case, from the practice of C.J.S., is disguised only to hide the identity of the couple; it illustrates how one psychiatrist works.)

When the Andersons showed up for treatment they had been married for seven years; Jonathan was thirty-two, Susan thirty, and their children, a boy and a girl, were five and two. Jon's complaint: "There's too much bitterness between us, not enough satisfaction. We fight about unimportant things." Sue's complaint: "I wanted a strong husband—but not someone as strong as my mother; she didn't let me have any freedom. I thought Jon was just right, but he isn't. He's stubborn, not strong. There are other things, too. He isn't fun—I can't play with him because he has no imagination. And our sex isn't very good. We would never do it at all if I didn't start it."

Jonathan, an engineer, had changed his job a year earlier in order to do work he enjoyed more. In the process, he took a sizable salary cut. Susan went along with this change even though it created money worries; the Andersons are committed to a high standard of living and whenever they can't pay the bills Susan reluctantly accepts money from her mother.

Susan's mother is a well-to-do woman in business for herself. Susan had worked for her before the children were born, and found her even tougher and more domineering professionally than she was at home. "Don't expect any favors," she often said. "You're not my daughter here, you're just another employee, no different from anybody else." But Susan *was* different; although she did her work well, her mother never left her alone but constantly singled her out for criticism and direction.

Now, with Jon's income reduced, Susan's mother was helping them, but not without nagging Susan to come back to work. Although Susan hated taking the money (which she insisted was a loan), she was determined not to subject herself to her mother's domination again by going back to the job. As her mother's demand grew stronger, Susan was becoming more and more angry with Jon.

When Susan came to the first therapy session, she looked and sounded like a flower child of the 1960s; she expressed her love for all mankind and her need to be true to herself, "one spirit with the sky, sea, and earth." She described herself as a folk singer and composer.

Jonathan talked about his new job, which involved the installation of security devices at a prison, and said that he was preoccupied with violence and given to morbid moods. It pleased him to think that "his" prison would be absolutely secure; he admitted that he was sadistically satisfied to know that the prisoners would be kept behind bars as they deserved because they had injured innocent people.

Susan, of course, was unsympathetic to Jon's views, and maintained that their different attitudes about crime, violence, and prison practices made for a running battle between them.

It took only a couple of sessions for the Andersons to become familiar with the concept of their private covenants, and they were both eager to write theirs out so that they could bring them to the next session. They did not show them to each other at home, but agreed that when they arrived at the doctor's office they would share them.

This is what they looked like:

SUSAN ANDERSON'S COVENANT

My Expectations of Marriage

Conscious: Verbalized

To have children.
To receive pleasure from my husband and children.
To be able to do my own kind of work and pursue my own kind of life.
He will give me financial and emotional security; he will be a balance wheel for me.
He will share my interests.
I will be safe and protected.
We will work toward a common end.

Conscious but Not Verbalized

I want to be completely at his mercy, to be his victim, so that I can feel; weak women feel, strong women don't feel.

It is good to be dependent on a strong man; it is my realization of my deepest being as a woman. A strong man can give me protection on an earthly level.

Beyond Awareness—until Now

You are a strong male, unlike my father.
I fear your strength and I want to destroy it.
If I encourage your strengths you might destroy me.
I need to be the strong and independent one.
I want you dependent and weak.

My Obligations

To be faithful.
To enjoy giving pleasure.
To care for the house and children.

JONATHAN ANDERSON'S COVENANT

My Expectations of Marriage

Conscious: Verbalized

You will be a good wife and mother; take care of the household.
You will be my companion and social escort.
You will be sexually faithful.
You will share shareable experiences.
You will help me relax and ease my tensions after the day's work.
You will be understanding of my personal frailties and prejudices.

Conscious but Not Verbalized

I want you to allow me to engage in activities you don't like.
I want you to be passionate and sexually demanding of me.
I want you to bear with my negative personality traits.
I want you to make do with my income without complaint.

Beyond Awareness—until Now

I want a wild, passionate, whorelike bedmate who will be verbal in lovemaking and accommodate my sexual fantasies.

I want an adoring and verbally complimentary wife who will massage my ego both as a person and as a male.

I want you to be attractive and teasing to other men—but never available to them.

My Obligations

Conscious: Verbalized

To support you to the best of my ability.
To be your escort and social companion.
To be sexually faithful.
To help you solve day-to-day problems.
To do heavy or unusual work around the house.
To be a father figure to the children.
To share, verbally and emotionally, my shareable experiences.
To accommodate your personal frailties and prejudices.

Conscious but Not Verbalized

I am willing to:
Allow you to engage in activities that I personally dislike—religious, spiritual, etc.
Tolerate your moodiness.
Avoid imposing on you sexually—although I will be available to you on demand.
Admit I don't earn enough to support you properly.

Beyond Awareness—until Now (*Trade-Offs*)

If you will behave with me sexually the way I want you to, I will:
Forgive and forget your past sexual experiences, although I'm jealous and feel insecure when I think of your former partners.
Stop asking you to refuse any more money from your mother because I realize that it's absolutely necessary.
Not pursue other women although I am attracted to the idea.

Both Susan and Jon were able to ferret out strong contradictory desires that had been beyond their awareness, things they didn't dare to—or simply didn't—think about openly before. This subconscious level of awareness is always a significant one, and in the Andersons' case, it led to expansion of their consciousness and to much greater understanding between them.

Susan learned that she was in conflict over control; she wanted to be in charge even while she wanted to be enslaved. She also found it hard to trust.

Jonathan's need for distance became clearer as time went on, but he picked up the first clues here, in his covenant; during the discussion he saw that his use of the term *shareable experiences* indicated that he saw some experiences as private, and that his "I want you to allow me to engage in activities you don't like" could mean little— or much.

Although these first covenants, as written, give no clear indication of it, the Andersons were actually very eager to make their relationship work and they had a good deal of understanding of as well as compassion for each other. The major problem seemed to be their different life and cognitive styles: Jonathan found it difficult to show love openly or to be close, and Susan was ambivalent about control and power, about Jonathan's closeness-distance, and about his passivity. Each wanted some independent activity, and each appeared willing to allow the other to have it—a good trade-off, if only they could do it in reality. Jon's sexual desires were acceptable to Sue, but only if he gave love and sex on her terms—that is, if he would be less passive and make her feel more wanted. The issues of money, support, and help with the children were important points of difference, too.

Both partners lacked security in adult femininity and masculinity, and each required strong reassurance from the other. Sue wanted to feel Jon's strength, to have him master her while loving and protecting her. She wanted to see him as a strong, loving father—but not as a weak father or a strong mother. She was angry, partly because she felt he *could* give her what she wanted but wasn't doing so.

As soon as they wrote out their covenants, Susan and Jon started to understand themselves and each other better. They saw how much damage they did by feeling injured and angry when each felt that the other had not lived up to the terms of the "deal." Susan was able to sum up her own terms as:

"I want you to make it possible for me to be independent and not to need anyone else to provide me with stability and security.

Whenever I feel overwhelmed by responsibilities I stop giving love and sex. I won't give you love if you don't give me status and security. If you *do* give it to me, and if you give me more emotional support with the children and the housework I'll be a loving—even a perfect—wife."

Jon had trouble with that statement because he thought he *did* give his wife strength, security, and freedom from material want:

"I do give her all that. It's just the damn money. It's not that I don't want to be fully financially responsible but I *won't* maintain our standard of living by doing work I don't want to do. Either we change our standard, or accept money from her mother, or Sue will have to work."

Sue said she understood his position and wasn't angry. But she did insist on emotional support and "togetherness"; he shouldn't act as if the children were hers alone. Although that's what she said, Susan really felt, emotionally, that a man who doesn't earn enough for his family and who expects his wife to work was weak—like her father. She knew that if she returned to work for her mother and could manage to stick it out, she would be very successful and would eventually own the business. Then she would be wealthy—but she wouldn't have any respect for her husband. In addition, *she* would wind up being the one who was doing what she didn't want to do. Those were her feelings, and although they were at odds with her intellectual ideas, she couldn't change the way she felt.

The Andersons spent many hours talking about their dilemma—and it *was* a dilemma, because each of them had a position based on deep psychological needs. Both the money and sex issues were symptoms, not real problems. Susan's problem sprang from her ambivalence: weak women feel, while strong women (like her mother) do not feel. Susan was therefore torn between wanting to be strong and wanting to be weak and taken care of. Jon's main problem came from his need to turn Susan into a doting mother. He needed reassurance, support, the love of an adoring woman who was sexually teasing with other men but who made it clear that she belonged to her husband. If she didn't behave the way he wanted her to, Jon would punish her by withdrawing. Sue's covenant demanded that Jon be strong and weak at the same time—a classic double bind. She withheld sex because that was her weapon in the power struggle. There was no way for Jon to satisfy her because her needs were contradictory.

After five therapy sessions, the Andersons recognized that if they were ever to solve the problems of their partnership they would both have to compromise and add some new terms to their covenants. By now, they knew, too, that eventually they would work out a single covenant for the two of them—but they weren't ready for that yet. First, they would rewrite their private covenants in the light of what they had learned about themselves and each other. For brevity, the three levels of awareness have been merged here:

REVISED COVENANTS

My Expectations of Marriage

Susan

1. Marriage means that the center of my life and Jon's is with one another and our children. We are a unit, self-sufficient and mutually supportive. My creative work is secondary—yet, I must have it. If Jon would cooperate, I wouldn't have to exclude one or the other.

2. The family unit is Jon, me, the children; it's not his original family, not mine.

3. I want him to be a gentle and understanding, yet firm, father. He should be concerned and help care for the children.

4. Family life will be run democratically and decisions about what, when, and how we do things

Jonathan

1. Sue and I are central; the children are secondary and are often an intrusion. Work is an important center for me, too. If pressed, I might choose my work over my family.

2. Same as Sue—but the children are secondary. The less we have to do with our original families, the better.

3. I will be a father image to my children. They must see me as strong, wise, and just. I don't want to be too close or involved in their daily problems.

4. I will take care of money and my work decisions. Sue will be in charge of family and social mat-

will be made jointly. I prefer that Jon make decisions about money and support; I don't want to know anything about it except that it's all OK.

5. Roles will be traditional. That makes me feel right and content. I'll care for our home and children; he'll earn the money and be my protector against outside forces I can't cope with.

6. Married people should like the same things, think similarly, share their feelings and thoughts. I feel uneasy and troubled when Jon won't accept things that are important to me—nature, spiritualism, the essential goodness of mankind, etc. If he can't do this, I don't know that I want to try to meet him on what he wants.

7. Married people should be sexually available to each other. If he gives me security and love I will be a model wife. But unless he wants me sexually and reassures me of my desirability I won't give him what he wants.

8. I don't want to be controlled now as I was by my mother. If I'm secure with my husband I can grow like a plant that gets the right nutrients, water and sun. Then I can be free to be creative. I will reward my husband richly for this: I want to and will take care of the house and children—with his help. I'll give to him sexually and make life exciting

ters—as long as I can depend on her to do what I want.

5. Same as Susan. But she shouldn't expect me to bail her out or fight her battles with some of her weird friends.

6. I'm a private person. I share only what I want to share. My likes and dislikes can—and do—differ from Sue's. I am separate and must remain so. Sue wants me to merge with her, but I won't and can't. That's definite!

7. I expect my wife always to want me sexually and to show it. She will be my refuge, my supporter. She will cater to my ego needs and will demonstrate how much she loves me and how sexual a man I am by making passionate love to me while telling me how wonderful I am and how I turn her on.

8. My wife must understand my needs—I'm special and should be catered to because I am a man and because I'm me. I will allow her some freedom to pursue her silly friends even though it threatens me and makes me anxious.

for him with my rich fantasy and imagination.

9. If I don't get what I need I won't give him what he wants. He must be strong enough to give me what I want; I don't want to be allowed to just take it because he's too weak to stop me. I don't want to have to be strong for both of us.

9. If I don't get what I want I won't give her what she wants. I must establish my authority so that there is no question about it.

10. I'll compromise. Jon doesn't have to join me in most of my interests as long as he allows me to pursue them.

10. I can't give her everything she wants because she would engulf and change me. If she gives me what I want I'll give as much as I can. I know compromises must be made. That's why now, I agree to accept money from her mother.

11. I don't think much about sexual fidelity. It isn't the important issue. Being there for each other when needed *is*. I would be upset if my husband couldn't give to me sexually but could give to someone else.

11. My wife must be sexually faithful to me. I feel insecure enough as it is.

12. We should be able to act out our fantasies with one another.

12. Same as Sue. But our fantasies can be different. I cannot and will not have the same fantasies she has. That isn't necessary in a marriage. A couple needn't be the same but should fit together properly.

After the Andersons had worked over these private covenants in their therapy sessions, they were able to draw up an analysis of the good and bad features of their joint expectations.

Positive

1. We both want the same kind of conventional marriage with both of us putting the emphasis on traditional gender-determined roles for ourselves.

2. Each may have independent activities—although Sue would like Jon to join in hers.

3. Each is willing to compromise and make some trade-offs.
4. Both want to stay together and to work on the relationship.

Negative

1. Our attitudes toward the importance of children are markedly different.

2. Jonathan is more distant and removed and sees this as a good thing.

3. Susan prefers a democratic system of decision-making while Jon is autocratic; Jon thinks that Sue only *says* she's democratic but often doesn't cooperate unless she gets her way.

4. Each wants the other to approach sex and love "unselfishly" and generously. There are genuine differences here: Sue wants love and security as well as assurance that she is desirable; Jon wants only to be reassured that he is sexually desirable.

5. Sue's conflict over whether she wants Jon to be weak or strong is a source of confusion and trouble; it is an important factor in the way the partnership functions.

6. Sue wants to be allowed to participate in the things that interest her—spiritual and humanistic movements, and her music—but expects and wants Jon to approve and participate. He refuses to do so because he is afraid that he will lose his sense of self. Sue wants him to like what she likes, think what she thinks; Jon can't stand the idea.

7. Sue tries to be guided by "shoulds" and "shouldn'ts" regarding control—but she isn't sure about it.

8. Sue and Jon both say that they will withhold from the other if they don't get what they want.

9. Jon is afraid of being controlled; he is threatened even by the idea of having the same fantasies.

10. Jon is very insistent on husbandly rights; Sue thinks he is hopelessly behind the times in this.

THERAPIST'S NOTES ON THE ANDERSONS

Childlike-childlike partners—two children in search of a parent.

For a man who considers himself a pragmatist, Jon is surprisingly ready to cooperate in the therapeutic venture with its demands for openness, exposure, and change. It's harder for him than for Sue; she's closer to her unconscious.

At present, the two live in an uneasy parallel relationship, each going his own way and each very unhappy and puzzled about why they are not more harmonious since they agree on so many of the superficialities of what they want from marriage. Harmony and growth are not ascendant, as each rigidly insists on having his own way in the particulars of living and relating. Ambivalence on the part of both in a struggle for power that each only half wants is a central negative force.

The following section is C.J.S.'s working hypothesis of the Andersons' covenants based on their inner needs. The material may be too theoretical for some readers; it is included here for those who are curious to know more precisely what and how one therapist can contribute to a couple's own effort. Italicized portions indicate my theoretical speculations regarding the Andersons' individual and couple dynamics.

WORKING HYPOTHESIS OF THE ANDERSONS' INNER NEEDS

Susan	*Jonathan*

Independence-Dependence

She wants to be dependent and independent but in different areas. This generates major conflict that she expects her husband to resolve for her. She wants to be her husband's slave and also to be free. *I do not accept her conscious formulation of this. I believe she wants a strong but loving and benevolent man who will protect and take care of her in return for which she will give him love, sex, children, and a warm family life. In turn he will further provide her with an ambience that permits her to be inde-*

He is clear about his desire to be independent—but this is a false independence. *Basically he desires a giving mother-wife who must fulfill his infantile need to make him feel good. In return he will then be a "good boy" at home and help out, share what he wants to share, be sexually faithful. A part of his contract that he cannot yet confront is that the women in his life are expected to give to him the goodies he wants while he lies back passively and is in charge.*

pendent in other areas. Thus there need not be a conflict in what she wants if her husband could give it to her; it is possible and a not uncommon quid pro quo on a more mature level. The master-slave or weak-strong polarization is therefore not an accurate assessment.

Activity-Passivity

She is willing to be active to bring about what she wants—active in deed as well as ideationally. In exchange for her active doing she wants his protection and care.

He is more passive than Susan but in a very aggressive way. He states clearly what he will do and that's it. He will compromise when he realizes he will lose the war if he insists on winning every skirmish; e.g., he agrees not to protest her asking her mother for money rather than cut down on their standard of living. He reacts more than he initiates.

Closeness-Distance

She claims she wants closeness, but her tolerance for closeness must be on her terms. She talks a great deal about closeness but protests too much. *Closeness to her is equated with controlling or being controlled.* She tries to bring Jonathan closer; i.e., to make him understand and to accept her style and cognitive approach. *He feels threatened by this and feels his integrity to be violated.* However, he can more readily accept their cognitive style differences than she. *Her attempts to control through taking away his defense—distancing operations—are done in a way that relinquishes her control to him be-*

He is wary of closeness, is too guarded. *Possibly he is fearful of his violent, infantile, and sadistic impulses.* He will make some gestures of closeness in order to remain distant but draws a line across which he stubbornly will not step. *As Susan said, he gives her the injunction "Don't be close," which frustrates her—robs her of a powerful weapon as well as a source of genuine gratification.*

cause he is strong enough to refuse to play the game on her terms. She then takes revenge with anger and her own withdrawal. Her closeness is often within herself—self-awareness in meditation. *On a deep level she does not fully comprehend or empathize with Jonathan.*

Power

She is clearly conflicted about how much power she wants to have and how much is permissible for her husband in order for her to feel safe—but basically she wants power and control. *She feels she cannot trust him with it. He is too alien and different. She is uneasy about the violence and sadism she senses. Her ambivalence contributes to their disharmony, as it both promises and withholds the mother-wife he wants whom he can control. Their struggle for power is a major preoccupation between them. Both enjoyed it early in their relationship, before it led to a deterioration of their marriage. When she has power she fears it and wants to hand it back to him—but then she can't trust him to take care of her: a terrible dilemma if one sees the alternative only in terms of her syllogism.*

He is not in conflict about power. He wants to have it but wants to delegate the active role to his wife so long as she does what he wants. His is a classical passive-aggressive personality syndrome. *The power and control question is crucial for them. He would want to exercise power as does a little boy who controls his parents. However, this tactic does not always work with Susan and he then becomes upset when he is forced to recognize that his omnipotence is threatened.*

Fear of Loneliness or Abandonment

This is a moderately important determinant of her behavior—particularly fear of the loss of the strong-mother fraction of her husband. It does not appear as a prime

He hides this fear well but he does cave in when Susan really pulls away from him. If she maintains her distant position he capitulates so that he can salvage the motivating force; the entire universe is her sisterhood. *Perhaps that is her ultimate defense against loneliness and abandonment.*

remnants of his fantasy of a blindly giving and doting mother-wife. If she threatens to leave him he threatens that his abandonment of her will be greater, swifter, and more terrible. *Thus he controls by stimulating her anxiety, not allaying it. What could be an opportunity to move positively becomes a power struggle.*

Level of Anxiety

Her level is overtly higher than his. She expresses it openly, is in touch with it, requests him to do something to relieve it for her. When he does not she focuses her anger on him or punishes him by not giving him what he wants. When too anxious she fears disintegration and protects herself by withdrawing, getting in touch with mystical forces that give her poise, calm, and a sense of being connected. Therefore, she feels that she can ultimately get along without him if she has to, but says she wants the children to have a father.

His anxiety is better defended against direct awareness and expression. It can most readily be measured by his sadistic fantasies, authoritarian position, and dogmatism. Unconsciously he is fearful of abandonment and Susan senses this fear and even uses it. He wants Susan to soothe his anxiety by ego massage and sexual activity, and in general to treat him like a beautiful male infant who is adored. Without this reassurance he becomes a cold person who knows he can hurt "mother" by withdrawing. However, this does not work too well with Susan because he cannot control her this way and now, when he uses this maneuver, she perceives him as her weak, ineffective father, whom she despises. At these times she then assumes the role of her strong mother—and then finds with horror that she has replicated her own parental situation. This is an unstable state that she can tolerate only briefly because she then insists that her husband be the strong mother-husband and take charge.

His superficial show of being the strong mother-husband also fails to stand up, as reality comes through to her despite her desire to see him as strong. She then swings back to anger and withdrawal and running away from him to be with her friends in the spiritualist movement. Once again in charge of herself, she returns and they square off for another round. He has learned from experience not to be too anxious about her spiritualism. It provides her with the necessities to stabilize herself and to serve him again for a while. Thus they go back and forth stimulating and relieving each other's anxiety. They are two children in search of a parent. Neither can accept a true parental role because they both need to be parented. *Therapy focused in on this seesaw very early and the quid pro quo approach proved helpful.*

Consolidation of Gender Identity

Her gender identity is female— but she is confused over whether being female means being like her strong mother or not. She wants to feel, but the strong do not have feelings—that is evidence of weakness. She still confuses being a "good female" with being a Hestia [goddess of the hearth], yet is conflicted by her desire to enjoy a whole gamut of activity independent from her husband. *How can she be Hestian and at the same time be strong, driving, and in charge? This would make her the "male" in*

His gender identity is male— but a beautiful, loved child, adored merely because he exists, *not* for anything that he gives or does. Ideally he would like to be married to a woman who is a giving "whore in the bedroom" and who adores him, a woman who would use her power and energy solely in his behalf. The idea of his wife working and earning money does not threaten him.

the family, like her mother. However, if she is to be independent she must be like her mother and have a weak husband. But she can't carry it off—it frightens her to be strong. To be strong would mean she could challenge her mother and that is a terrifying idea. Besides, she is a child. She sets it up as an either/or situation without full appreciation of the fact that both she and her husband can be strong and accepting at the same time; that a person can care and be cared for, can be weak or strong and can like the spouse taking over in some situations while he or she takes over in others. The possibilities of sharing, and of powers shifting back and forth between them, are lost in the anxiety generated by the recognition that one's mate has the same flaws as oneself. The problem of passing control back and forth is one of the important ones for them to work out together. It is significant that gender role, control, independence, etc., all become interrelated aspects of the same overall ebb and flow within their marital system. Homosexuality is not an abhorrent idea to her but she prefers a male sex partner. She does not experience erotic feelings toward either weak or strong women.

Characteristics of Sex Partner

She wants a partner who will be turned on by her and who will make intense spiritual and physical love with her. Unless he instigates

His ideal sex partner resembles her picture of herself acting sexually with other men. Physically he finds her face and body beautiful it in a loving way she does not want sex. It angers her that her husband does not keep his part of the bargain in the quid pro quo (interchange). She feels this is illustrative of what often occurs. Also, she feels she was wanton and "sold herself" sexually before marriage because she felt she had nothing else to offer. She does not feel that way now and resents his demands. Physically he is fine sexually for her and can arouse her when he wants to. There are no sexual dysfunctions. It is his lack of sexual initiative and assertiveness, as well as his not creating a loving ambience, that puts her off and makes her feel undesirable. She stated at one point: "I, too, want to be loved for the person I am, not just a pussy." She wants him to be more aggressive and not to be stopped by her rejection of his sexual advances. In exchange she will become sexually giving.

and voluptuous, just what he wants. He is angered at her "refusal" to be wanton with him and to fit into his whore-in-bed fantasy. In exchange for her doing this he would not contemplate other women and would take care of her "to the best of my ability." *Again this is an equivocal and not reassuring statement.* He wants her to accept him sexually; he says he stopped taking the initiative sexually with her because she rejected him. She states that he accepted her "no" much too easily and that she wants him to override her objections and take her.

Acceptance of Self and Others

She basically questions her own worth as a person and as a woman. *Therefore the man who accepts her must be defective too. This produces a perfect stage for the acting-out of problems based on her low self-esteem, particularly as her mate reinforces the negative attitudes she already has about herself and is very parsimonious about offering recognition for her positive contributions and attributes.*

Although he assumes he is an adorable male infant he also fears he is not a match for a "real man," including any of her previous lovers. This lack of acceptance of himself as an adult male contributes greatly to his need to control and structure his world so that he always appears to be in command. *He is strong enough to choose the areas he wants to be "weak" in. These are not necessarily the ones she wants—e.g., she wants him to*

be strong in making money, in de-
siring her sexually, in being able to
tolerate her going off by herself, in
being less passive. He is strong in
doing the work he wants to do.

Cognitive Style, Energy Level, Intensity, Absorption, Enthusiasm

Susan's cognitive style is open and intuitive. She allows data to flow in and around her and then makes a decision based on her visceral feelings. She writes her lyrics and music and lives this way. This style is markedly different from Jonathan's. She finds it difficult to accept his way and keeps trying to push him into her style. She feels hurt and alone because he won't (can't) join her in her seemingly unstructured approach. Yet, she follows logic and sees to it that the essentials are taken care of for herself and for her husband and children. She has a high energy level, intensity, absorption, and enthusiasm and expects the same from Jonathan, which he does have, but unfortunately not in the same areas as she.

Jonathan's cognitive style is very logical and precise. He, as a proper engineer, surveys all situations, collects information, sifts it through and organizes it into its appropriate categories and weights, and then arrives at a practical decision in accordance with the "facts." He has learned that his wife cannot do the same and will condescendingly tolerate her "escapist, spiritualist, and humanistic activities." This difference in styles makes for communication problems. In addition, each has become impatient with the other's style and thinking. *Because they know they will not change each other's position they tend to cut off communication and are too impatient to listen, each believing that he/she knows what the other will say.* Energy level, intensity, absorption, and enthusiasm are high. He does not care much any more about the direction of Susan's energies so long as they are not too threatening; ultimately she does what he wants.

APPARENTLY EXTERNAL PROBLEM AREAS

These are the complaints that often bring a couple into treatment. They are usually symptoms of something more basic than the couple's conflicting terms as expressed in the first two categories.

| Susan | Jonathan |

Communication

Susan appears to be quite open and direct in what she does and does not want, even when these are contradictory. She *appears* to ask for what she wants, but in reality many of her messages are not clear, and often are double-binding because of her ambivalence. She is in good contact with her feelings but allows negative ones to pile up and may then explode without adequate thought to the consequences. She can express love and tenderness as well as anger.

However, when she feels disappointed she does not state what she wants but expects Jonathan to know. She will give subtle signs, which are not likely to be understood or even perceived, and then finally blow up with anger when she has accumulated a series of what she considers refusals to respond on Jonathan's part.

In summary, Susan is in touch with her feelings but often does not clearly communicate what she wants.

Jonathan is open in what he wants in terms of events and things but is not in good contact with his feelings and hence cannot express them directly. At times he expects his wife to know and to fulfill his unexpressed wishes. He finds it difficult to express love but can express anger readily. Many of his communications come through in an authoritarian and blunt way that arouses the ire of his wife. Early in their relationship she thought this was an evidence of his strength, but she now sees it as weakness and is angered by it. His hostility is often expressed indirectly and in a subtly sadistic way that only thinly masks his underlying anger.

When Susan gives her mimimal signals he does not perceive them or, if he does, usually misreads them. Instead of asking for clarification he "guesses" what she means, usually taking the most negative interpretation available.

In summary, Jonathan, in contrast to Susan, is not in good contact with his feelings but does communicate clearly what he consciously wishes to communicate.

Interests

She is an artist and interested in matters of the spirit and in her own work as well as her family life. She had expected him to be concerned

He is interested in himself essentially. He wants to tell her about his work—but only those aspects that he feels enhance him. He is not in-with her sphere of interest and to agree with her opinions. She becomes angry and disappointed and feels unloved when he disagrees with or can't comprehend her point of view. She is not especially interested in his work because she has not found a way of seeing how it relates to her basic philosophy of life. Hence she is somewhat suspicious of his work, which makes him angrily defensive.

terested in what she does but is willing to live and let live. She may pursue her own interests as long as he is not deprived of her wifely services. If he is, he retaliates angrily.

Lifestyle

All living matter is one. She wants her life to be free, spontaneous, spent with gentle people, music, singing, dancing, conversation, nature, and without worry about money. She is outgoing. She is willing to compromise, i.e., wants to do all of the above with Jon but will settle for his not punishing her for sharing with others if he will not join her.

He is closed in, ordered, a planner. He likes some people as long as they do not threaten his supremacy. He dislikes being close to nature, prefers motels to camping out. He is very agreeable about spending money if they have it. He goes along with her activities to some extent but is threatened as he comes to realize that the people to whom she is drawn are not like him and he fears he may eventually lose her. He therefore tries to rein her in, which angers and depresses her and makes her pull away.

Families of Origin

Her strong mother is a source of problems for her and for them— Sue is very ambivalent about her mother. She uses her mother as the yardstick by which all human qualities are measured, both good and bad. She regards her father as a sweet nonentity. She wants her mother out of her life. Therefore she resents Jon "putting her" in a

He fears her attachment to her mother and is jealous. He regards her mother as having too much influence in their daily life. But he is partner to perpetuating the situation by not either making more money or insisting they live within his income. He consciously made the choice to accept the situation, rationalizing that he did so for Sue position of asking her mother for money because she feels that she is the one who must pay for this.

and the children. His family presents no current problems to either except for the effects of his early relationships with his mother and father. At times Sue resents his father's past indulgence of him and his mother's coldness and distance. His father is dead and his mother lives in another state and is not an active force in their lives, except historically.

Children

They both agree that the children are primarily Susan's responsibility. She gets angry, however, when Jonathan does not carry out his part of the quid pro quo; i.e., to relieve Susan's worry about money and security so that she can do the things she wishes to, such as work with her music, join in activities with spiritualist friends, etc. She resents his distant stance with the children, which he considers providing "a proper father image." These are minor conflicts over child-rearing practices but he usually abdicates to her in this area.

Money

To her, money represents power and freedom, as amply illustrated above. She becomes anxious as the realization strikes her that money is short. Rather than cut down she takes the easy way of accepting money, and therefore control, from her mother.

Money means the same things to Jonathan but he is not overtly concerned about material matters and feels confident that financial needs will be met one way or another.

Values

There is nothing to add here to what has been covered above. There are many areas of agreement in addition to some profound differences.

Friends

Friends represent independence to her. She claims she would like to

He has few friends of his own. He is willing to share those he does share, but she did choose a husband who can't share her most significant friendships.

have with her but she finds his choices dull or obnoxious. It is all right for her to have her own if they do not threaten his sexual possession of her.

Roles

She is willing to follow traditional gender-determined roles if she gets what she wants in return. She resents his not fully accepting responsibilities of his role as money-maker.

In his honesty and bluntness he at times appears an exaggeration of the dominating and yet ultimately complying husband. Roles are clearly gender-determined for him ("I will help with the heavy work at home, if I can") but he wants to define his responsibilities and brooks no discussion about them. His intransigence is frustrating to her.

At this point, I was ready to help the Andersons work out a single covenant to replace the two private, somewhat conflicting covenants they had. When you are ready to do that you will find, in most cases, that it is quite possible to do it without professional help. Naturally, you may proceed in quite a different fashion. Your approach will probably be far less theoretical, more intensely personal. We'll come back to working out one covenant in a later chapter.

7

The Sexual Covenant

Until fairly recently, almost everyone—therapists included—took for granted that the kind of sexual relationship a couple had was representative of the couple's entire relationship. The pioneering contributions of Masters and Johnson opened the way for sex to become a respectable and appropriate subject for clinical investigation. Even those professionals who had worked with couples for many years often failed to understand how two mates' sexual satisfaction related to their total relationship. They assumed that the two areas were essentially similar. For a long time psychiatrists and related professionals have stressed the individual's psychology and functioning or physical health while paying little attention to the way partners interacted. Now, that emphasis has changed.

As more and more therapists began to offer conjoint sex and marriage therapy to couples, they began to gather a different, more accurate kind of information. Whereas formerly the therapist usually heard from only one partner about what took place sexually between mates, now many therapists hear both partners' accounts. As a result, the professionals have made a discovery: They see that some couples with good overall relationships have poor sex—and, much more surprising to most people—some couples with poor relationships have excellent sex.

This will not be so surprising to the reader who has an understanding of covenants. Because of our different behavioral profiles and different inner needs, we have different sets of expectations about what our responsibilities are. All partnerships have areas of agreement and areas of conflict, and sex can fall into either category. Since sex is extraordinarily basic and yet extremely complex, it calls for special attention. Most couples in effect (although not always literally) have separate sexual covenants; these may or may not parallel their general covenants in points of agreement or conflict.

As a result, the quantity and quality of sex as well as love and commitment may vary within a relationship. All couples who have good sex have a good total relationship some of the time; some couples who have good sex have a good total relationship all the time; but other couples who have good sex do not always have a good relationship all the time. And conversely, some couples who have poor sexual relationships are close and loving in other ways.

For a majority of couples the two relationships do mirror each other. The same power struggles and defenses, the same ability or inability to be close, the same capacity to enhance or spoil one's own or the partner's pleasure at the moment of fulfillment, the same demands, the same interdependent, childlike, or parental attitudes may prevail in sex as in other areas.

For other couples, sexual interaction is a thing apart; the partners behave quite differently with each other sexually than they do generally.

Nora and Ben Brody disagree about almost everything. Nora is a volunteer worker at an art museum and deeply involved in the art life of her city. Ben is in the wholesale hardware business and likes to boast that he doesn't know a Rembrandt from a Warhol. He calls his wife's friends "pretentious phonies" and is barely civil when he is forced to associate with them. Nora, on the other hand, finds Ben's friends (and Ben himself) "ignorant, loud-mouthed, money-grubbing boors." For the most part, Nora goes her own way and spends several evenings a week at the museum or art galleries. On those evenings Ben sees people on business, or meets "the boys" for a regular twice-weekly poker game. Often on such nights the Brodys do not meet until bedtime—but when they do, one of two major patterns of behavior emerges. Sometimes they find something to fight about; then they try to outdo each other with complaints and insults, shouting until they finally get too sleepy to go on, and, still muttering, they fall asleep. Other times, without any conversation at all, the Brodys make passionate love. As adept at pleasing and being pleased sexually as they are at tormenting each other verbally, they leave each other limp, exhausted—and totally satisfied.

Nancy and Frank Hudson are quite different. They seem to have everything in common—the same tastes, the same friends; they enjoy the same movies, music, books, and food, even work for the same company, and come from the same Midwestern town. They are deeply committed to each other, communicate openly, and have good times together. They are so loving and affectionate that most of their friends think of them as the ideal couple. And they are—with one exception. They hardly ever make love any more. It bothers both of them a little bit since it doesn't seem "normal," and yet it is the one thing they never discuss. On the rare occasions when they do have sex, they enjoy it.

Jean and Henry Caldwell demonstrate a third kind of behavior. They have been married for a number of years and have had a consistently good and loving relationship. Unlike the Hudsons, they have a high degree of sexual interest, but for some time their sexual encounters have generally wound up in frustration for one or both of them. Although they have bought all the books, gone to all the lectures, and tried all the positions, Jean almost never has an orgasm and Henry often has problems maintaining an erection. They are thinking now about sex therapy, and it might be a good idea for them. It is likely that they can learn to function as well sexually as they do in other ways. However, there is a small possibility that it will do more harm than good to the rest of their marriage. Occasionally, after successful sex therapy, couples begin to encounter more general disharmony than they had before; this surfaces when they can no longer use sex as a cover-up for their other problems. Usually, it is better not to push problems under the carpet—but each couple must make that decision for themselves.

Although sexual functioning can be modified by many influences, there is a great variation in the way people respond. For reasons no one understands entirely, some people function well sexually even in a hostile relationship (although that may or may not be their preference); their ability to enjoy sex is not impaired even when they have been involved in a nasty quarrel. They seem able to separate their sexual pleasure from upsetting situations that would make others lose all interest in sex. These people are, perhaps, a fortunate minority. For most, the interweaving of love and commitment with sex is variable and perplexing. It would be ideal if we all had a full measure of all three of these desiderata, but it rarely works out that way. The proportions are different for different people, and often they are different for the partners in one relationship. These differences are reflected in their covenants.

Some sexual covenants may include a spoken or unspoken agreement that one partner will relieve the other's guilt about sex by taking the initiative, allowing the other to remain passive. Or a man may play into a woman's fantasy that the penis is hers, not his; in exchange, the man may use fantasy to satisfy an unexpressed homosexual or transsexual thread within himself that does not require complete or continuous fulfillment. Such complexities are not uncommon.

In the Andersons' covenant, Jon wanted "a wild, passionate, whorelike bedmate who will be verbal in lovemaking." She needed to feel loved and wanted before she could give him that. She wanted him to be so strong that she would feel like his victim. They were at a sexual stalemate until they were able to compromise and play out each other's fantasies to achieve a more mutually satisfying sex-love relationship.

Lois and her husband Anthony Stone, an English professor, entered therapy with serious complaints about their marriage and their sexual relationship. They were not sure whether or not they wanted to stay together, but they felt that they would be in a better position to make the decision after they had made some effort to discover what was wrong. Since they insisted that their sex problems were a major source of dissatisfaction, I (C.J.S.) encouraged them to work out a single couple covenant that would express clearly what they wanted from each other and what they were willing to give in exchange.

After they had done so, I asked the Stones to bring in their private covenants—and promised to keep them confidential until they were ready to share them with each other. I wanted to review them myself so that I would know how best to counsel the couple. When I had finished reading them, again for my own clarification, I drew up a working hypothesis of what I thought the unconscious portions of the Stones' covenants were.

The covenants and the hypothesis emerged as follows:

THE STONES' SEXUAL COVENANTS

Conscious: Verbalized

Lois	*Anthony*
1. I can help you sexually and will be glad to do so. I'll take care never to humiliate you.	1. You are sexually free and experienced and you can help me. I am sexually inadequate, inexperienced, and vulnerable. I expect you to help me and to teach me.
In exchange for the above:	*In exchange for the above:*
1. You are able to help me professionally since you are a professor and a gifted writer while I am a beginner and insecure. I expect you to help and guide me, to the best of your ability, so that I can develop professionally.	1. I can and will help you professionally. I won't be competitive with you.
2. I am often depressed and emotionally up and down. I expect you not to reject me for this.	2. You are often depressed and emotionally up and down. I will not reject you but will try to be understanding and helpful.

Conscious but not Verbalized

1. You expect me to help you with sex. I want to and I will. I will make it appear to others that you are a sexually adequate male.

In exchange for the above:

1. I am anxious and afraid that I can never make it alone professionally. I can't compete. I'm helpless and I'm jealous of your professional status. I want you to help me so I can be as good as you and as good as other people. I want to feel acceptable.

2. I'm afraid you'll leave me because I'm so depressed and irritable; you're really too good for me. I'm not very good—so you must not leave me. I don't really want you to get better sexually; your insecurity about sex is the only thing that gives me a hold over you.

1. I want many other women but they won't want me unless I improve sexually. You represent my only chance for sexual freedom. I expect you to give it to me in exchange for everything I do for you.

In exchange for the above:

1. I'm willing to help you professionally, and I won't compete with you. However, I will try to get you to go into an area different from mine because your competitiveness makes me uneasy.

2. I'm willing to reassure you, but it gets really tedious. I hope you mature soon. I would like it if you were as strong as my sister—my ideal.

THERAPIST'S WORKING HYPOTHESIS

Levels beyond Awareness

Lois

1. I am nothing, but I want to be supreme. I can achieve this only through you. You will be strong and powerful for me so that I can use your power to control, dominate, and compete. I will submit to you in exchange for the male power that I lack.

2. Females are passive, males

Anthony

1. I am afraid to be sexually free. I want other men to envy me, but I'm afraid of them. I can only be sexually free with your permission and protection. I expect you to make me free—not just with you, but with all women. I will make you powerful in return. I will let you dominate me.

2. Women are inferior. I want to

are active. I want to destroy you for being a strong, active male. It makes me feel inadequate. I won't abandon you if you let me destroy you.

3. I'm excited by the thought of your having sex with other women. I'll make you free if you'll have other women for me.

4. I'm afraid you'll abandon me if you compare me to other women. You mustn't have other women. If you don't, I'll make you sexually free in exchange.

5. We must be close and intimate.

6. We must remain distant and separate.

7. You must agree to *all* my terms. In exchange, I won't leave you.

dominate you. If you dominate me I'll be angry at you and will despise myself for being so dependent. I won't hurt or abandon you if you'll let me dominate you and put you in an inferior position.

It is easy for anyone reading these covenants to recognize at once that they are both full of contradictory terms. It is no wonder that the Stones had such a stormy time together. Sex was "good" only when Lois was completely in charge, but Tony would then rebel by becoming impotent. The Stones' differences were beyond fixing, and as a result of their therapy they were able to face this. Since their battles and sexual dissatisfaction, Lois's episodes of rage and depression, and Anthony's anger toward her were unceasing, they soon decided to divorce.

When he came to my office some months after the divorce, Tony reported that he and Lois were now more amiable toward each other. He himself was much happier; he had a good relationship and good sex with a woman friend although he felt that he was not ready to be deeply involved with anyone. He did not know what was happening to Lois personally since they did not talk about intimate matters.

But Lois soon called for an appointment, too. She had had some sexual experiences with another woman and was feeling much better and more at peace with herself. She realized that she felt more harmonious with women than with men although she wasn't sure that she wanted to commit herself to a lesbian life. Still, at the moment, her new relationship seemed right to her.

This couple illustrates some of the complexities of the sexual clauses of covenants and how they relate to other areas. If the Stones had not been unconsciously so ambivalent they might have been able to stabilize their relationship but, as it was, it would have been impossible for them ever to make their peace with each other.

There are a number of ways in which people can pursue sexual gratification and conscious and unconscious sexual wants are incorporated in the sexual clauses of all individual covenants. Some people use them profitably and find apparently ideal sex partners this way; they can live happily ever after if they stick to the rules of their game—that is, if they can accept the relationship with no need to destroy it.

Another course is taken by someone who *tells* him or herself that a chosen partner is the right one, even while entertaining some doubts about whether or not this partner is sexually ideal. Such ambivalent people now have several choices. They may refuse to see any flaws in their partners and continue stoutly to deny that there are any. They may see the flaws but convince themselves that as soon as some other conditions change (when we marry, when we have a child, when we're a few years older, have more money, and so on) the flaws will disappear. Or they may treat a potentially ideal partner in such a way that the partner *cannot* be sexually fulfilling; they see to it that they spoil whatever is good. In more extreme instances, some spoilers do not ever get a chance to spoil since they cannot select a satisfactory sex partner in the first place; such men and women are driven by masochism or defensive needs to choose partners who will doom them to frustration.

Within this general framework, tremendous variation occurs in the qualities of "good" sex and sexual partners. Much depends on how partners interact with each other—what their covenant terms are and how they deal with them.

RULES OF THE SEXUAL GAME

As with other areas of individual covenants, the way two partners establish and adhere to the rules of their game creates the essence of their sexual behavior together and decides whether or not sex is fulfilling for them. If it is not, it is often because their interaction is faulty, not because there is something inherently wrong with one or the other of them. As with other parts of individual covenants, each partner has conscious and unconscious terms that the other may not have agreed to or does not fit into a complementary way.

Couples who are not in the habit of talking about their sexual relationship in detail can begin to establish open communication by discussing their last sexual experience. You and your partner could take turns describing, step by step, exactly what happened. Note what each remembers or leaves out and where there are real differences of fact or feeling in your accounts. Here is one possible agenda: Who initiated sex? How? What signals were given? How were they interpreted? Received? Answered? Specifically what kind of foreplay took place? How did each of you feel? What was your mood? What was the overall ambience? If possible, recall how each of you felt at every point along the way. It may be difficult for you to discuss these things at first, or it may be exciting—or both.

Now shift to more generalized areas: Are you individually and together free and open in sexual play? What does each of you like? Dislike? What, if anything, is forbidden? Do you use fantasy? Do you play out roles together? What would each of you like sexually from the other? What is each of you willing to give? What excites each of you? What is the wildest fantasy each of you has?

Some important covenant terms include what attracts you sexually, how you like sex to be initiated, how often you want it, what you think are appropriate sexual roles for men and women, what place sex holds in your life, what enhances or inhibits your sexual pleasure, and who or what may be included in your sexual relationship—in short, what exactly you want your sexual activity to consist of. Do you want your mate to inhibit or free you sexually? To be a playmate, a parent, or a peer? Do you use sex to gain some advantage or control elsewhere in the relationship? Do you use it as a trade-off for something in another area?

Let's look now at some of the specifics of individual sexual covenants.

Sexual Attraction

Most people find the physical appearance of a mate important; it is a key factor in initial attractions. That does not mean that the partner must be particularly beautiful or handsome, only that he or she must meet some personal standard. A few people pay little attention to appearance; still others make choices that are highly idiosyncratic. Often, these seemingly odd choices result from transference: A tall woman, for example, may be attracted only to short men—not because she wants to dominate them, but because her father, whom she adored, was a short man.

Smell and personal hygiene can be very important among these expectations. Some people have strong olfactory reactions, others do not. Those who do may use a partner's odors as rationalizations to avoid intimacy; conversely, they may find that odors are greatly stimulating. The antiseptic, hygienic, nonsmelling man or woman of the advertising industry is not necessarily the most sexually attractive to everyone. Our growing knowledge of pheromones which apparently can be isolated, not just from insects, but from the vaginas of healthy young women, supports the conclusions of many observers that humans, like lower animals, are affected sexually by olfactory as well as by aural, visual, and tactile stimuli.

Personality and character factors are bases for attraction, too, especially those that fit the inner needs of the partner. And the behavioral profile that the mate either displays or is maneuvered into can add to or detract from sexual excitement. For example, one woman was generally pleased by her partner, a take-charge kind of man. She enjoyed his aura of power and competence and, as a preliminary to sex, would begin to act like a child, forcing her mate to be more and more paternal. Then, as their sex play continued, she would invariably provoke him in some way so that he became angry. At this point she would become very excited sexually and beg his forgiveness, in a frightened, childish way. "Daddy" would then forgive her by accepting her advance. Both partners found this scenario extremely exciting.

You can enhance your self-knowledge considerably by asking whether your attraction is determined by a sense of being loved, by wanting to conquer or be conquered, or by your need to be accepted and/or warmly understood. Subtle interpersonal styles and needs are often of great importance in creating and maintaining attraction between two people. While many have relatively catholic tastes, a few people limit their choice of partners to those within a narrow range of specific personality, character, and physical characteristics. These specifications can change, too, as one goes through life—often creating problems in a long-term relationship.

Initiating Sexual Activity

Give some thought to how sexual activity usually begins in your partnership. Some couples work out elaborate seduction rituals each time; others are very direct, simple, and straightforward with each other.

Sex signals, and sensitivity to them, are worth a study in their own right. Some couples are equally ready to give and/or receive pleasure; others always rely on one or the other to make the first move. Some men and women are afraid to be the initiators because they find rejection too painful to bear; they don't understand that the rejection of a sexual overture isn't necessarily a rejection of the person who makes it.

Signals may be clear or extremely subtle. Sometimes they are so subtle that they are self-defeating. One woman complained extensively about her husband's lack of sexual interest. When pressed for more detail, she explained that whenever she hoped they would have sex, she simply inserted her diaphragm but never mentioned it or made any overtures. When asked why, she answered that there was no need for any announcement or further action; her husband certainly realized that she was staying in the bathroom longer than usual. When the husband was asked if this was the case, he said with some surprise that yes, of course, he *did* notice that his wife stayed in the bathroom for a rather long while on occasion. However, he always assumed that she was staying in there because she was trying to avoid him, so he simply rolled over and went to sleep.

Although most couples believe, intellectually, that a woman should be as free as a man to initiate sex, many women are still too afraid of rejection to take the chance; when the man makes the approach, they are safe because they know they are desired. On the other side of the coin, while most men like being approached, some do not because they feel that they can never refuse even when they want to.

My (C.J.S.) practice does not indicate an increase in impotence among men today because more women are sexually aggressive— although there has been a fair amount of speculation about this in the media. A liberated, affectionate, and secure woman isn't any more apt to be hostile or inconsiderately demanding with a man than a liberated, affectionate, and secure man is apt to be with a woman. Unfortunately, there are some people of both sexes who still abuse whatever power they may have.

It is sometimes difficult for one partner simply to accept a gift of sexual pleasure and gratification—an act of fellatio or cunnilingus, for example—from a mate who for one reason or another does not feel like becoming sexually aroused at the time. The spirit of giving and accepting sexually can be one more reflection of a couple's loving relationship, but it is hard for some people to receive pleasure without feeling guilty and pressured to reciprocate immediately. One man became terribly upset because his wife didn't feel like having sex on a particular evening but told him that it would make her feel good to make love to him. He could not accept her offer, and instead of understanding that she was being loving, he felt rejected. It took a fair amount of thought and discussion before he learned to value himself sufficiently to accept his wife's loving gesture without feeling guilty.

Male versus Female Roles and Activities

Although stereotypes of "proper" male and female sexual behavior are fading, it is often difficult for adults to throw off the training they received as children. A man who was raised to believe that women are passive, shy, and "pure" may think he wants a woman who is thoroughly egalitarian about sex. However, when he finds such a woman he may, in spite of his intellectual convictions, be dismayed to discover that he considers her too aggressive and "unwomanly." Or he may find himself thinking of her as a "whore." Each couple needs to explore what the two of them want and enjoy, and they need to express their desires openly; sexual exploration and expression are part of an ongoing process, since desires may change from minute to minute, encounter to encounter, mood to mood, year to year. It is important that both partners always feel secure and free to be sexually experimental and to follow their fancy with each other.

Either partner may have rigid ideas and feelings about kissing, touching, and fondling—whether it be breasts, vagina, clitoris, penis, testicles, anus, fingers, toes, ears, or any other parts of the body. They may have very set ideas about the need for, or the exclusion of, cunnilingus, fellatio, anal intercourse, various coital positions, and so on.

For some couples the man may usually play a dominating role, the woman a meek and submissive one—or vice versa. If either is true in your case, you might ask what your feelings are about such roles. Must they be constant, or can they be flexible? How are dependency, closeness-distance, power, and other inner needs reflected in your sexual covenants?

Frequency

The amount of sex two partners would like to have can differ, and can also vary over time. How do you decide on the frequency of sex and sex play? Do you avoid sex because of a lack of security or a fear of "inadequacy"? Sometimes partners collaborate to avoid sex; they may do so because of boredom, anxiety, gender-identity questions, lack of sexual attraction, physical illness, depression, or because there are other problems in the relationship.

When one partner wants more sex than the other, the couple may resolve the matter by a trade. For example, the one who wants less sex may agree to make a special effort to accommodate in exchange for some like favor. If avoidance is a result of sexual dysfunction the couple should see a marital therapist who is also competent in sex therapy.

The Importance of Sex

Sex may play a minor or an important role in a couple's life, and its significance may shift at different times. Married couples may engage in sex to have children or mainly for pleasure. Some couples use it to relieve anxiety and tension, or as a refuge from the outside world. Conversely, sex may reflect the tensions and struggles of their life together.

For some couples, sex is valued as the ultimate in intimacy and openness. Couples might ask themselves if they both feel the same way about this or whether one is more open than the other. Does their sexual relationship fulfill their needs for infantile care and pleasure as well as for adult love and sex itself? Does one want only holding and petting (parental love) without sexual passion? Do control and power flow back and forth in a smooth manner? Or does one partner's covenant demand that one or the other always have control? *Everything that adds to understanding adds to intimacy.*

In exchange for whatever each of you gives sexually, what do you expect in return? Can or will you meet each other's wants? Are your covenants the same? Complementary to each other's? Conflicting?

Sophie and Ezra Salem were a childless couple in their late twenties who came to therapy with the complaint that they were growing apart. Ezra said he was subject to depressions that made him withdraw; Sophie, at first, had reacted to his withdrawal with anger, later with resignation and hopelessness. But they believed that they loved each other, were generally compatible, and wanted to make their marriage work.

When they gave their sex history they both said very emphatically that, mechanically, sex was fine; they both always had orgasms during coitus. But Sophie felt that, emotionally, their sex wasn't good at all. For several months she had avoided it except on a few occasions.

Sophie had had sexual experience with other men before she married and had valued the time right after orgasm as a particularly close period. "It's when I can be most open," she said, "but Ezra turns away from me just when I want most to snuggle and talk." Ezra confirmed that this was so but said there was nothing he could do about it; he felt an unbearable need to get away as soon as the sex act was completed. He was aware of Sophie's unhappiness whenever this happened; it made him feel threatened, as if she were trying to control him by clinging. But there was nothing he could do now in any case because he was feeling too depressed to have any interest in sex.

When the Salems began to work on their individual covenants they became aware, for the first time, of some areas in which they were in direct conflict. Ezra was extremely fearful of any real closeness; he liked sex for the physical pleasure it gave him but he didn't want any affection connected with it. On reflection, he recalled that his mother had been a very seductive woman who used her sexuality to manipulate men. Ezra was frightened of being manipulated by Sophie, so whenever she tried to draw him close to her he escaped by withdrawing, turning his anger into depression.

Sophie, for her part, realized that she had tremendous anxiety about being rejected. The most important aspect of sex, for her, was not physical pleasure but the assurance that she was loved. Without intimacy, sex was worthless to her, and she preferred to do without it.

Because the Salems' differences sprang from their inner needs and could not easily be resolved, couple therapy did not seem to be the best treatment for them. Instead, they each began individual therapy; in time, Ezra stopped confusing Sophie with his mother and

Sophie learned to be more secure—especially when Ezra became able to be a little less remote.

What or Who Else is Welcome in Your Sexual Relationship?

Is there anything you like to include to make your sex better? Perhaps you like to build a fire, light candles, play music; you might enjoy erotic literature, pictures, movies, or sexually stimulating conversation. Some people like to indulge in fantasy—either silently or aloud—and some enjoy playing out a fantasy. You might find that you can enhance your pleasure with body oils, vibrators, dildos, or special clothing. Perhaps you *do* all the things you like and have tried those you thought you might like. But perhaps you have only *thought* about them and have never dared to suggest them.

Most couples have a period of intense sexuality at the beginning of their relationship, but after a time, as the intensity wanes, they may feel the need for more variety and stimulation. If they use a little imagination—and trust each other enough—they can readily discover new, pleasurable activities. For some, it is exciting and intriguing enough to gain an increasingly deeper understanding of each other, to discover new mysteries and facets within themselves. Others, just as loving, need other stimuli to sustain sexual passion. One couple plays out variations on a "danger of being caught" fantasy. They make believe they are students hiding in a supply closet at school; adults who have just met on a half-empty jet liner; a doctor and patient in the examination room of a busy office. Other fantasies that are often acted out center around call girls, threesomes, master-slave situations, or mild sadomasochistic play.

In addition to objects and fantasies, couples can decide whether or not any other people are actually to be admitted into their sexual relationship. Most marriages and intimate arrangements are predicated on monogamy. Even those "liberated" people who believe they can easily handle their partner's having an outside affair are often very much surprised, when it happens, to find that it is not easy to handle at all. There is most often a strong emotional response that is usually negative. Even when the reaction isn't completely negative, a known outside relationship always changes an original one. Each couple should decide how they feel about monogamy, and not take for granted that it is equally important to both of them.

In practice, few couples today may regard an extramarital relationship itself as an automatic reason for divorce, but an affair can still stir up a great deal of trouble. If an outside alliance doesn't conform to their covenants, most people are likely to see it as a danger signal rather than a death knell—and it *is* frequently a hostile act directed against a mate. Many can deal better with a partner's casual sexual encounter than they can with a significant emotional relationship that has no sex at all. Many men and women claim they would not be bothered by their spouse's having a brief encounter when they are geographically separated, but they do not want to hear about it. An emotional relationship with someone else *is* less tolerable to a couple's system. Most people find a partner's relationship with someone they both know particularly hurtful. Personal reactions vary. It is hard to know how each of you feels about the matter of "infidelity"; your partner's feelings may help to shape your actions.

How one feels about the inclusion of a third person (or any number of people) in the couple's own sexual activities is also a highly individual matter. Many people who enjoy the fantasy of threesomes don't like the reality. For others, the addition of a third person may be necessary to pleasure. The same thing is true of partner-swapping or group sex.

Experiments in both of the latter have been going on for a number of years. Some couples try one or the other and stay with it; they find that the experiences gratify their needs and fantasies without endangering their relationship. Or, one may see the activity as important in his or her covenant and the other may be able to go along with it. Some couples find that they benefit from variety and sharing the experiences; this becomes a bond that holds them together. After experimenting, others find these activities disruptive, without rewards, distasteful, or upsetting, and so they give them up.

These possibilities are outlined because, all too often, people take for granted that the sexual components of their relationship will be limited to their own preferences. The main purpose of this chapter is to point out that sexual covenants can be very varied, and should be verbally explored together. As you work on your own covenant, ensure that the sexual provisions are as comprehensive as you need them to be.

Couples who have special problems centering around sex might do well to work out individual sexual covenants before they try to work on their general, more comprehensive mutual covenant. The simplest way to do this is the way Betsy and Jay Adams did theirs. The points are expressed informally and are perfectly straightforward:

BETSY'S SEXUAL COVENANT

What I Like

I like to make love after we have had a particularly close, romantic evening. An evening when we go out to dinner, or go dancing, or some evening when we're at home and we eat by candlelight and play music. I begin to think about it then, and I know you do too, and it's like being on a date and just waiting for it to be time to go to bed. Then I'm in the mood long before we begin, and I know it will be very good.

I like you to hold me and kiss me for a long time before we do anything else. That's what you used to do before we were married—we used to hold hands in the movies, then come home and sit on the couch and kiss for a long time before we went to bed. We never do that any more.

I like to hang back and act reluctant—even when I'm not.

I like you to act aggressive, as if you really want me so much it's the most important thing in the world.

I like you to tell me that you love me, that we belong together forever. And to tell me I'm pretty and exciting.

I like oral sex—but I like it better when you do it to me than when I do it to you.

I like to have sex about as often as we do—but only when I feel like it.

I like lots of foreplay and like to continue it until *I* feel ready for intercourse.

I like you to take a shower and shave, and put on your silk pajamas that I gave you for Christmas.

I like you to notice how nice I smell, and what I'm wearing, and if I just washed my hair.

What I Don't Like

I don't like it when we have hardly spoken to each other, or when we've been cross, and suddenly you grab me in bed and think I'm ready for sex just because you are. I never am, when it's like that.

I don't like you to rush me into intercourse before I'm ready. Sometimes when I want more foreplay you act bored—and that does me in.

I don't like you to kiss my breasts unless you ask me; sometimes they hurt, and I don't like to have to talk about it then because it spoils my mood.

I don't like it when you need a shave. It makes me feel as if you don't care enough about me to bother.

I don't like to use a diaphragm or to be the one who always has to be responsible for contraception. Our sex would be better if you were willing to have a vasectomy. It makes me angry that you won't even discuss it seriously.

I don't like even the idea of anal sex and it upsets me when you keep asking me about it. That makes me angry, too.

I don't like to make love in the morning. I always feel as if my teeth aren't brushed (they aren't) and I usually have to go to the bathroom so that all I can feel is my bladder. And I worry that the children will get up.

I don't like you to use vulgar sex words; they don't excite me, but do the reverse.

I don't like to have sex when you've had too much to drink. You're always very selfish then, and I feel used.

I don't like you to talk about having sex with other women, or make jokes about getting one of my friends to join us. You know that I would never consider anything like that and I think you do it just to annoy me.

I don't like you to urge me to try new, crazy positions. They make me feel self-conscious and stupid—but I feel like a bad sport if I say "no" all the time.

What I Wish

I wish you were more affectionate when we're *not* making love.

I wish you wouldn't make jokes about my prudishness in front of others.

I wish you would use the vibrator on me sometimes as part of foreplay, or when I don't have an orgasm. And that you'd stop saying no battery-operated toy can do anything you can't do—because you're the one who told me to buy it, and it was hard for me to do, and we've never even tried it.

I wish you'd let us try marijuana sometime; everybody says it makes a big difference, and maybe it would help me get over some of my inhibitions.

I wish you'd stay awake longer after sex, and talk to me for a long time.

I wish that once in a while you would give me a nice massage, rub my back, and my legs, and my neck, and do it for a long time—without expecting anything else to happen. Every time you promise me a massage I know I'm going to have to "pay off" even though I feel relaxed, and sleepy, and content, and really don't want to do anything except sleep.

JAY'S SEXUAL COVENANT

What I Like

I like it when you're clearly interested, get very excited, act enthusiastic.

I like you to let me know that you're in the mood—not make me try to find out, as you usually do.

I like you to go to bed without anything on.

I like oral sex. Both ways.

I like to have sex in places other than bed—the living room, outdoors, in the car—like we used to once in a while. And I like to do it at different times, not just bedtime.

I like the way you always smell so clean and nice and perfumy.

I like you to get on top of me and let your hair hang in my face.

What I Don't Like

I don't like to have to hold back, go according to your timetable; it feels unnatural, makes me lose the urge.

I don't like your straitlaced approach to sex, as if it can only be done in certain proper ways at certain proper times.

I don't like your silence.

What I Wish

I wish you would be more abandoned—act as if you really *like* it, not just *let* me.

I wish you would give me more clues; I never know whether I'm pleasing you or not.

I wish you wouldn't be so rigid about anal sex. I don't know how you *know* you would hate it if you've never tried it.

I wish you would be more willing to try new positions.

I wish you would be willing once in a while to do something really crazy—like do fellatio in public places, under a coat or something, so people can't tell what's happening.

I wish you would be willing to try a threesome.

I wish you would stop nagging me about a vasectomy; I know it would make me feel castrated, and the "facts" have nothing to do with my feelings about it.

I wish I didn't feel so often that you're doing me a favor.

I wish you enjoyed getting boozed up and having a rowdy time.

I wish you would wear a black-lace nighty some time.

I wish you could use sexy language once in a while; it would drive me crazy to hear you say some of the words.

After Betsy and Jay made these statements they began to talk about many things they had never discussed before. They began to see that although there were some ways in which they couldn't fulfill each other's wishes, they were able to make enough trade-offs to improve their sexual satisfaction considerably.

Jay did agree to use the vibrator after Betsy agreed to buy a black-lace nightgown. The first time she wore it she found, to her surprise, that she enjoyed parading around in it and looking at herself in the mirror. On her own initiative she put on high-heeled sandals, jewelry, and makeup. The sight of herself was so amazing that she looked like a different person; as a result, she acted differently, too. Not exactly wantonly, perhaps, but much more freely than ever before. They were both delighted with the experience.

And Jay found, to his surprise, that the vibrator relieved him of a great deal of pressure. Every once in a while he was able to enjoy not trying to hold back—and then the gadget *could* do what he couldn't.

Betsy and Jay made several other trades after that, and their sexual relationship improved immeasurably. Encouraged by this fortuitous outcome, they decided to go on to the other areas of their relationship and begin to work on a full couple covenant.

Unless you feel that sex is a particular trouble area, there is no special reason to work out a sexual covenant on paper. It is worthwhile, however, to *think* it through, to talk it through together, and to bring the knowledge you have gained to the forging of your couple covenant.

8

The Couple Covenant

By now you have the means to be aware of your own individual covenant, including its sexual areas. You know that it deals with your expectations in your relationship—what you want from it; your inner needs; and any outside areas that seem to create problems for you, those special arenas in which you and your partner may choose to wage your battles. You also know that in addition to the covenant terms you talk about, there are others that you do *not* talk about, and still others that are unconscious.

By this time, too, you have undoubtedly given some thought to your partner's covenant; perhaps you have guessed many of its terms, maybe the two of you have discussed them. In either case, your two covenants are not absolutely identical; that would be highly unlikely. It is possible, however, that your covenants are harmonious on most major points. If so, your covenants are *congruent*. Another possibility is that your covenants are *complementary:* although different, they combine well. The third possibility is that your covenants are in *conflict*—they disagree or clash on many issues.

Similarly, your own private covenant may have terms that are congruent, or at such odds that the covenant, on scrutiny, is not workable. Internal conflict within individual covenants is a common cause of strife since it leads to ambivalent messages and behavior.

Ideally, then, each person's covenant should be harmonious within itself and for the most part either congruent with or complementary to a partner's. Covenants that approach this ideal evolve with ease into single covenants to which both mates subscribe freely. It is not necessary—or even desirable—for all the terms to be identical; it *is* important for both partners to know what their differences are and to be able to accommodate in such a way that they can resolve these differences—or at least keep them from causing serious discomfort or dissatisfaction. When dissatisfactions do occur—and they must—mates should be able to express their feelings clearly. If they are familiar with their feelings and are able and willing to communicate them well, they can almost always talk their way through to some equitable solution.

Obviously underlying problems can never be resolved unless both people understand what they are. And yet many couples fight about money, sex, in-laws, children, and even who takes out the garbage when those are not the real problems at all. Often the real problem lies with impulses, wishes, and feelings that are subliminal. It is difficult to find these out for yourself and harder still to discuss them with a mate who may confirm your belief that these factors keep you from being an ideal person. They must surface; otherwise one deals with hundreds of brush fires rather than the source that ignites them.

The objective is, of course, to turn areas of conflict—whether they are within yourself or between the two of you—into areas of congruence or complementarity. You may do it by means of trade-offs, or in other ways. But remember: *you will never resolve every single difference.* It is unrealistic to believe that any couple can be free of any differences at all, and so, unless your conflicts are particularly destructive, you will have to learn to accept and live with a certain number of them. It is likely that more relationships founder because of unrealistic, unspoken expectations than for any other single reason.

It may be possible, then, to improve your relationship—but not to make it perfect, since perfect relationships exist only in fantasy.

Working toward a single couple covenant is a highly plausible and likely means to fulfill your individual and joint goals. The *process* of working together toward this covenant is not only a means to an end but an end in itself, since a single couple covenant, like the perfect relationship to which it points, can be approached but never fully achieved.

A covenant is a living and significant concept solely in terms of a specific intimate partner. Most of us think we know what we want of a relationship before we enter one, but as we become involved, interact, and form close bonds with someone, our ideas begin to change imperceptibly. We forget qualities we formerly considered indispensable, and the other person's qualities become woven into our new ideal. As we learn to communicate with each other, we begin to establish new standards, roles, patterns of behavior, even common myths. To our surprise, we discover all sorts of abilities, traits, and needs within ourselves and each other that we never knew were there.

Most people function somewhat differently in different relationships. Even those who have been married before, and are sure they know what they want and do not want in a new mate, are frequently surprised by the extent to which they modify their terms in the crucible of a new marriage. As two people become significant to each other, they automatically begin to work toward a single covenant. As a relationship deepens, each partner (even if unaware of doing so) constructs, then elaborates on, a rudimentary covenant. If the relationship is a very good one, the pair may, without ever knowing it, work out an excellent couple covenant on their own.

But few can do it as well unconsciously as they can consciously. Most of us need to work at finding the fine print in order to expose the hidden clauses. Even then, no one can hope to adhere at all times to the letter and spirit of the emerging pact. Instead, we need to learn to negotiate with each other. This is an invaluable skill; once mastered, it can serve well for a lifetime, since the terms of a covenant, the goals of a relationship, change constantly as they reflect constantly changing life situations.

All relationships call for quid pro quos—you do this for me and I'll do something you want. It may seem materialistic or even crude to introduce the concept of trade-offs into a love relationship, but all intimate relationships need them to survive. Trading off is not debasing. It encompasses altruism, concern, responsibility, and love.

A couple covenant can be thought of as analogous to a business contract; it is absurd to expect both parties to be overjoyed by every clause. One accepts a less advantageous clause at the top of the page in exchange for a more advantageous one farther down. The objective is for both partners to know about and to *agree* to the same clauses, to find the overall contract congenial.

Here the analogy ends; unlike a commercial contract, a covenant can never be signed, sealed, and delivered to stand forever unchanged. Covenants *must* change, as life changes. Conflicts are resolved and new conflicts arise, and each time they do a covenant has to be renegotiated so that the emerging areas of conflict can be brought back to congruence or complementarity.

CONGRUENCE

When individual covenants are truly congruent they almost always result in good relationships, particularly when those subtle, formerly unconscious, expectations are fulfilled for both partners. To illustrate one aspect of congruence, studies have shown that marriages most often succeed (that is, endure) when spouses come from similar social backgrounds. Of course it is difficult to determine whether the marriage of the boy and girl next door is more likely to last because of social pressure or because the two share a cultural heritage. Although it seems likely that congruent values do tend to keep these couples together, there are not enough recent studies to provide reliable evidence on this question.

Congruent covenants are most characteristic of equal-equal, companionate-companionate, and parallel-parallel partners. The Waldens, equal-equal partners, have congruent covenants:

Melissa and John Walden are both college instructors who make every effort to insure that each has the chance to work and to achieve as much as the other. When their baby was born they arranged their schedules so that each parent works half a day and takes care of the baby and home the other half. They share all responsibilities, and each brings in half of the family income. They have equal opportunity to advance in their professions.

In spite of their outward independence, the Waldens are dependent on each other in a variety of ways, and they cater to each other in these as well as in their needs for independence. They have a circle of warm, close friends among whom they are highly respected as individuals and a couple. They meet one another's deepest psychological needs and function effectively as a unit.

If the Waldens' situation sounds ideal, it is—and it is extremely rare, as well. Genuine congruence in so many major areas is exceptional, but it is not necessary—if both partners are mature enough to respect each other's differences. The most common areas of congruence are in cultural values and mores, where the couple "speak the same language." But if they are not somewhat alike in their psychological needs as well, they may have trouble in achieving a rich and durable relationship. However, a basically congruent couple can do well even with some significant differences. The Russos are a case in point:

Tony and Marion Russo are both from second-generation working-class Italian families; they were brought up on the same block in New York City's Little Italy and now live only two blocks away from where they began. Everything about them—their relationship itself, their lifestyle, their total ambience—still has an old-world flavor. Their neighborhood is their village; they know every shopkeeper by name and have at least a nodding acquaintance with everyone within a four-block radius. They entered therapy because they were in conflict over how to deal with one of their children.

Marion was a high school graduate and Tony had dropped out after two years. Eventually, he got an equivalency certificate and a job in the city sanitation department. He had a strong need to be an important person at home, and his wife catered to that. Because of their similar upbringing, Marion understood Tony's need for respect and was able to give it to him without losing respect for herself or for her role as a wife. They were compatible in every way except one—their philosophy of child rearing. Marion was a firm believer in education; it was important to her that all three children go to college. Tony failed to see the need for college and interpreted Marion's insistence on it as a criticism of his own lack of schooling.

The Russos' conflict centered on the oldest child, a fifteen-year-old boy; his recent behavior impelled his parents to seek help. Tony Jr. had been failing most of his courses and was frequently truant; he had become a hanger-on to a group of tough older boys who had recently formed a club he hoped to join.

He was, in fact, acting out much of what he sensed as his father's masculine protest against a rapidly changing world. Little Italy, invaded by large numbers of non-Italians, was no longer the secure island it had been. Having grown up where it was "right" to be a male supremacist, the boy was reflecting his father's uneasiness in a society where equality was now contemplated, if not lived, and where women often seemed to have the upper hand. Although he was not aware of it before therapy, Tony Sr. had some troublesome questions about himself vis-à-vis his wife's strength.

The real problem was not easy to uncover because the Russos were, as they had always been, devoted to each other and their family. But times were changing, and their lives were changing; the one thing that was not changing was Tony Russo's covenant. He wanted everything to stay the way it had always been; he was fighting desperately to maintain a status quo that could not be maintained. He saw that his wife was changing along with everything else and his private world was threatened on a most basic level.

As a sanitation worker Tony had security, a relatively good income, and a position in his community. This position still held up well even though other friends and neighbors had become middle-class business owners, a few were wealthy, and several had children who had become professionals. Marion was sensitive to this and knew that their "village" within Manhattan would not hold out much longer. It would remain their own secure home, but the children would move out—when they were old enough—from the old world into the new and they would be assimilated. The Russo children would not be Italian-American adults, but Americans. It seemed to

Tony that his wife was betraying him with this. He accused her of saying, in effect, that the life he had given her was not good enough for their children. There was no way to hold back "progress," but there seemed to be no way to make Tony Sr. accept it. And yet he had to accept it.

It was not easy. It took the children themselves and the parish priest to help convince Tony that if his son were to succeed in *his* world, he would have to go to college. Tony Sr. finally came to see that it was up to him as a father to encourage his son to break away from the old ways and accommodate to the new. As he helped his son to change, Tony changed himself. He finally realized that his wife had never demeaned him; she really was well satisfied with their position in the community, even though the children could not be.

Through an understanding of the covenant principle, Tony was able to accept his wife's looking for a part-time job. He could deal with the fact that she wanted to grow, to move with the times in order to feel good about herself, and that her desire to do so was no reflection on his earning ability or his masculinity. Eventually he would even acknowledge her feat in bringing about so much change within the family, and he would express his gratitude to her.

The Russos were successful in adapting as they did because they had great respect for each other's dignity. They came to feel consciously and realistically secure about themselves as individuals and as a unit.

Introducing the Russos to the concept of covenants was exciting because, like many others, they had long had an excellent couple covenant even though they did not know it. They had been able to make minor modifications in it throughout their marriage, but when a basic reevaluation was called for, they needed help. Because their covenants were essentially congruent, they made the most of the help and became an even closer couple than they had been before.

Not all relationships that appear to be congruent are truly so: some are only superficially congruent, while on deep emotional levels there is no congruence at all. This explains the "model marriage" that suddenly explodes when one partner can no longer stand the hypocrisy of the pseudomutual life the couple leads.

COMPLEMENTARITY

There are more good, or even excellent, relationships based on complementarity than on congruence. Partners who truly complement each other—which means that they fulfill each other's neurotic needs as well as their "healthy" ones (those areas listed in Category II of covenant terms, pages 56–59)—frequently have successful, long marriages. Since it is difficult for most of us to become free of neurotic needs, we are fortunate indeed when we find someone whose neurotic needs dovetail nicely with our own. And if we can complement each other in some positive ways, too, so much the better, since we are most gratified when we are least dependent and anxious.

In good partnerships based on complementary covenants, a couple's neurotic and realistic needs fit together in ways that work to the advantage of both of them. They resolve their conflicts differently from those who know and accept each other's abilities as well as limitations, and work out trade-offs. Instead, a complementary couple creates a relationship in which each partner *uses* the traits or needs of the other—not in exploitation but in reciprocity.

Graham is shy, uneasy with new people, while Lucy is life-of-the-party—gregarious, outgoing, adventuresome. But Graham is far more intellectual than she; he is scholarly, thoughtful, and well-read, while Lucy is none of those. They have a natural complementarity that satisfies them both: Lucy constantly makes new friends, invites people to dinner, accepts invitations. Graham enjoys being part of socializing and knows that on his own he would never be capable of initiating or sustaining it. But once an evening is under way and he has overcome his initial shyness, he is an excellent conversationalist and engages the most interesting people present—the very people Lucy most enjoys but with whom she could not establish rapport on her own. Together they lead a fruitful life that satisfies them both. Of course socializing is only one facet of their life together. In some areas they are congruent and in others they have arrived at quid pro quos.

Complementary relationships often provide a combination of talents that make the partnership work well. We all have different needs, abilities, and proclivities and complementary covenants allow people to make full use of their special traits and needs. This is most apparent in those romantic-romantic partners who "complete" one another, in parent-child relationships, sadomasochistic combinations, and so on. Complementarity allows some psychologically and even organically incomplete people to maintain mutually gratifying relationships.

This is not to say that all complementary couples are essentially neurotic. They may be relatively healthy people whose character traits enhance each other's.

Gilda and Newton York have an excellent marriage in which she makes all the major decisions and sets their style with her own special taste. She manages their savings, decides when to buy a new car and which car it should be. Gilda chose the colonial house they live in; she opted to sell their contemporary furniture and furnish it with early American antiques. Gilda and Newton discuss what concerns them both, but Newton usually finds Gilda's opinions agreeable.

Newton is quite content with the way Gilda manages their life together, and admires her easy and quiet way of getting things done. He respects her—as she does him; he excels in his professional life— and they are devoted as well as loyal to each other. Although they prefer to do things together, both are able to function well alone. When Newton is away on his frequent business trips, Gilda is busy and comfortable, and though Newton often wishes Gilda were along to see particularly interesting sights, he enjoys restaurants, museums, friends or relatives in whatever city he is visiting.

Gilda simply accepts it as a fact of life that she is relatively assertive while her husband is somewhat passive. Newton accepts it, too. Although they have reversed the stereotyped roles to some extent, their untroubled attitudes make their relationship a good one. If Newton were ambivalent about his passivity he would feel angry, disgusted, or inadequate as a male; he might turn his self-denigration against his wife and blame her for it. Similarly, if Gilda resented Newton's passivity, or the responsibilities he "made" her assume, the marriage would be marred.

The Yorks are fortunate in this regard; often people in similar situations let themselves be torn apart by internal conflicts. If Newton, with his inner need to be dependent on his wife, were ruled by cultural values that deemed a man less than a man because he was dependent, he would be in grave conflict. Whenever he gave in to his need he would lose respect for himself. Whenever he acted independently he would be acting against his wife; he would become anxious that she might stop loving him. As in any double-bind situation, the conflict could immobilize him, or make him act impetuously in defensive, defiant, or inconsistent ways. Whatever the outcome he would displease himself, his spouse, and everyone who knew him; any move he made would be a losing one. Since a self-imposed double bind is as destructive as one imposed by someone else, complementary partnerships are successful only when they are relatively nonambivalent for both mates.

In Chapter 5 we saw a couple, Gregory and Eleanor, who both feared abandonment but who defended themselves against their anxiety in different ways; each thought the other would be the savior. This kind of superficial or false complementarity often brings couples together—to their eventual sorrow. They choose mates for the positive qualities they think the other has and that they themselves lack: strength, social ease, decisiveness, drive, and so on. During their courtship they are so eager to please that they manage to maintain the fiction. But in time the truth is bound to surface, and the bubble of illusion breaks. How common it is to hear "If I had had any idea what he/she was really like I never would have married him/her."

Even then, disillusioned partners often have no inkling of what went wrong. If they examined their covenants, they might find that both had selected a partner for qualities he or she lacked. They endowed one another with qualities they wanted to see. (In some instances, partners do play roles, trying to be the idealized person the other one wants.) They probably found ways to compensate for their shortcomings and managed to hide them for a long time. But finally, when repeated hints and then overt pressure failed to get the mate to supply the missing quality, the deception was exposed.

This kind of marriage is like one between two poor people who both pretend to be rich. They are initially happy, each believing that they will never have money worries again. But then the rent comes due. He expects her to pay, she expects him to pay. He says he's a little short this month; she says that's funny, so is she. The game can go on only so long; the landlord will insist that the rent be paid. At this point, both partners feel betrayed, bitter, and thoroughly duped.

In real life, the structure of a falsely complementary relationship is beyond the partners' awareness and so they blame their pain on a variety of other causes. They can begin to remedy their situation only when they are ready to confront the real issues in themselves and each other. Recognition of similar sources of anxiety often leads to a united effort.

CONFLICT

Although the very term *conflict* has a frightening connotation, it should not; it is not necessarily negative. The existence of negative clauses in a couple's covenant does not mean that the relationship is doomed. On the contrary, conflict often leads to growth, a result of identifying, confronting, and dealing with (not necessarily resolving) significant differences. What *is* destructive is ignoring conflict or passively giving in to demands in order to avoid it. By comparison, bringing differences out into the open, acknowledging them, and then coping with them is very profitable.

But there are some kinds of conflict that no one can profitably handle. If, for example, one partner has inner needs that are absolutely necessary to his or her security, and if the other is absolutely unable to satisfy them, the pair will not readily find a solution to their troubles. They may seek therapy in an effort to change or they may decide that they are basically incompatible and separate. Or, if one partner has needs that *no* single individual can satisfy over a long period of time, that person may opt for an alternate lifestyle rather than a committed relationship.

Although it remains the common pattern, not everyone is able or wants to fit into a marital or quasi-marital relationship. Fortunately, in contemporary society it is possible for nonconformists to choose a pattern that suits them better. Some of the possibilities are communal living, living alone, maintaining two residences while in a committed relationship, serial monogamy, multiple simultaneous relationships, homosexual relationships, and many more.

Seeking another lifestyle is an unusual outcome of conflict. Much more frequently, the discovery of conflicting covenant clauses has a remarkably healthful effect on couples. Although it may cause some initial discomfort, this is, at worst, like opening an abscess in order to heal it. At best, it is an exhilarating experience that brings two people close.

When conflicts center around inner needs, it is helpful if both partners can discuss their expectations and wants openly. This is hard for many because they fear exposure or do not know what they want. Learning what your own needs are calls for self-examination and listening to your mate's view of what they are. You will learn more and more about your own individual covenant. In addition, a certain amount of good comes from simply knowing each other's needs and expectations. Many partners, even without trading or negotiating, will modify their attitudes or positions when each understands clearly what the other wants. As partners discuss their individual covenants they are, then, working toward a couple covenant that is free of secret clauses.

ARRIVING AT A COUPLE COVENANT

When your mate has worked out his or her private covenant according to the same guidelines you have used, you are ready to begin to work together—but do *not* rush into instant revelation! Do *not* exchange covenants. You may even want to promise each other that you will make no effort to "snoop" at the other's covenants, but will merely exchange information as you see fit, at a rate and in a way that makes you both comfortable. If you do not trust your partner to respect the privacy of your covenant, destroy it after you have written it out. The fact that you have done the work will make it possible for you to remember most of it.

Obviously, any two mates who are working together to improve their relationship are not likely to sabotage the effort before they have fairly started. But caution is necessary if one has pressured the other into working out a covenant. *You should not do this.* If either of you is reluctant, you need a professional guide to keep you from doing more damage than good. Only those couples who are in wholehearted accord on really making an effort should continue.

Here is *how* you proceed. First, make an appointment for a work session, a definite time when you are likely to be uninterrupted and when you are able to be relaxed and comfortable. Set a time limit for the session and agree that you will stop at the end of the time and make an appointment for your next meeting. An hour or two per session is probably enough.

If you cannot decide which one will begin, you might toss a coin. Start with the clear understanding that you will not reveal anything you are not ready to reveal at this time, and that neither of you will put pressure on the other. The work is pointless unless you are both honest—but it would be foolhardy to expose yourself before you feel safe in doing so. *If you create too much anxiety the project will founder, so be gentle and easy with each other.* Cooperation and caring are the keywords. If you feel anxious, remember that your partner is as anxious as you are—maybe more so. Be aware of each other's feelings; make every effort to make each other feel better, not worse. If you can put your partner at ease, you will be more at ease, too.

When both of you are ready, one should start reading the beginning of his or her covenant. Remember to reveal only as much as you want to at this point. If you wish to skip some items, do so. When you have read your first item, ask your partner if he or she will read you a corresponding item. Each of you should keep a tally sheet so that you can see your points of agreement and disagreement, your gratifications and disappointments.

Do not try to cover too much territory in the first session. You may cover only the first few expectations of the relationship, you may cover only the first one, or you may finish the entire category. Do *not* try to cover more than one category in any one session. Whenever either of you feels that one of your expectations has not been met, talk about it. Be specific. State exactly in what way you think the other person has failed and what your feelings about it are. Deal in the present. If you believe that you were let down sometime in the past, but that that situation has been remedied, don't waste time on it.

When you have explored the first category, go on to the next, until you have finished. If you kept some things back the first time around, you might want to go through the list a second time. If each of you still has some secrets, don't worry about it; as you grow closer through the covenant work you will feel able to reveal more.

When you have come to the end of your covenants and studied your tally sheets, you are likely to have learned a great deal about yourselves, both individually and as a couple. You will have a clearer idea of the kind of mate each of you really wants and how well satisfied each of you is with the other. You will know why you want the relationship at all, which partner has which powers, what makes each of you anxious—and what you do when you feel anxious. You will know what kind of self-image each of you has; you will be more aware of your approaches to problem-solving, your ability to communicate, tastes in friends, attitudes toward children, values, and more.

You will, all along the way, have amended each other's errors and misapprehensions about one another—and you will know each other (and yourself) better than you ever have before.

When you have reached this point, you are ready to begin negotiating your couple covenant. First, write down all the congruent items—those in which you are in complete agreement. Next, write down those in which you complement each other—in which your differences serve each other's needs and work to your benefit. You may be pleasantly surprised to see what a good combination you make. Many couples who have frequent quarrels or dissatisfactions are heartened to find that in the majority of important areas they are in agreement and that their troubles stem from a few relatively minor sources. (It's like getting a bank statement and discovering that you made a mistake and actually have an ample balance when you thought you were nearly broke.) Such good news will leave you feeling emotionally rich and in the best possible mood for further communication and closeness. You will realize that you have a solid basis for going forward together and can dare to trust each other more and more.

In this mood of optimism and intimacy, you are in the best possible condition to list your areas of conflict. It is in this list that your real work lies. Now, like heads of state or presidents of giant corporations, you will "wheel and deal" to resolve your differences; you will make the best possible bargain, but you will take care to keep negotiations open and to wind up with a "deal" that leaves both parties satisfied.

You might prepare to negotiate by doing some homework. Write down a list of trade-offs you are willing to make: "I will promise to be sexually faithful if you will agree to have a second child." "I will try to be less passive, to take more responsibility, if you will help me more with my sexual problems, pay attention to the details I have outlined in my sexual covenant." "I will make an earnest effort, even when I find it difficult, to communicate freely and openly, if you will be kinder to my parents." "I will stop complaining about your spending money if you will be more emotionally open with me." "I will never again threaten you with abandonment if you will allow me to see my friends once a week without argument."

Try not to wage bitter battles over the trade-offs. Remember that you are *negotiating* on a high level, not fighting a war. Don't expect to resolve every conflict. *There is no relationship that is without conflict*. Do the best you can. No matter how much or how little you achieve, you are likely to be closer than you were before.

Most important, don't be afraid that if you agree to give something, you will be stuck with the decision forever. No covenant can last forever because life circumstances are constantly changing, and as they do, your covenant has to change, too. Working on your covenant will become a way of life, something that you will never finish, but a means that is an end in itself. The nature of the ongoing process will be discussed more fully in the next chapter.

Since every person, and hence every couple, is unique, no two couples will encounter the same challenges in working on a covenant, nor will any two go about it in precisely the same fashion. You will discover the way that is best for you.

It should help you, however, to know how a therapist might steer you in the right direction and assist you along your way. Although you will not be able to do everything by yourselves that you could do with a professional, you can probably do as much as you need to. The couples who seek help are those who are already in trouble, the ones who cannot find their own way— or may not want to. Most couples can do well enough on their own.

COUPLE THERAPY

The remainder of this chapter is from a book C.J.S. wrote for other professionals (*Marriage Contracts and Couple Therapy*, Brunner/Mazel, 1976) which explores how one psychiatrist works with couples. The material has been adapted very slightly to eliminate some of the technical language. It offers several "tricks of the trade" that you can adapt to your own use.

Early in treatment I usually start to orient clients toward forming a single covenant in order to enhance their relationship. Often this is, at first, implicit, as the three of us compare the terms of the two covenants they have verbalized or written out. Mainly the road we travel toward the goal of one couple covenant *is* the work of therapy. The terms of the covenant must be the choice of the two mates, not mine. I try to be a guide, a facilitator, a remover of roadblocks. I draw their attention to problem areas as well as to those that are congruent and complementary. I suggest ways of changing their behavior to each other, and I interpret their dynamics to them when I think that will help. I relate the present to the past—to their parents' marriages and their relationships with their parents, to their roles in their original families, to their interchanges with siblings and how this may affect their current behavior—and to other life experiences when this is relevant. I ask their consent and cooperation in making changes in their current system.

The therapist's role is somewhat similar to that of an experienced fishing guide who has contracted to help his clients accomplish their goal but cannot guarantee success. The guide tries to set up the most feasible and expeditious conditions for the venture. He uses his accumulated knowledge and experience. He knows the habits of the fish in his locale. He attempts to make his clients as comfortable as possible on the outing but they must realize that fish cannot be caught from the terrace of a tenth-floor suite at the local Hilton hotel. And that the trip may be arduous, inconvenient and even painful at times, but that the rewards are worth it—if they really do want to catch fish. It is the guide's duty not to steer the boat into white water that is too dangerous for his clients to handle. He does not take his clients through rapids that will endanger their lives. He points out that there may be other fish in safer pools, or that perhaps this couple will decide to end their expedition together.

Using the private covenants, and the interactional scenario (the rules of their game), the objective is to achieve a joint covenant instead of the unilateral ones with their hidden and not-agreed-upon clauses. The therapist uses his skill to help reduce the number and the noxious effects of newly discovered, as well as already known, conflict-producing terms. Neither spouse will necessarily find all clauses to be optimal in their couple covenant. It must involve quid pro quos, as well as negative and positive complementary clauses that may or may not wholly please either partner. But they must at least be workable for each and accepted without rancor or a sense of capitulation. Both spouses must have the ability and motivation to fulfill their parts of the terms.

To arrive at such a single covenant (whether it is spelled out as such or not) the couple usually has to become aware of at least the most troublesome areas of their individual covenants. Verbal agreements in regard to one issue may be made but cannot be carried out for long when there is an underlying conflict in another sector. The problem area may then have to be bypassed and the anxiety reduced in some appropriate fashion; alternatively, the re-remote underlying causes (often having their origins in childhood) may themselves have to be dealt with.

Once approximated, the single couple covenant has to be reviewed periodically by the couple, since goals and needs change in the life of the couple, and for each person.

Communication

There is no need to elaborate on the role of communication. Communication between mates, verbal or nonverbal, is the means, the message, and a goal for couples in or out of therapy. It is also the therapist's instrument. Elucidating covenants so that they come fully to light, as well as working toward a single covenant, is intelligence transmitted by communication.

Goals

Goals are essential in treatment and also offer an approach to rapid initiation into therapy. An ordered, stepwise procedure is to set simple goals and then move on to others when the first are attained. Covenant information guides the couple and the therapist here, and involves the clients as full participants in deciding what they want. It helps to assure them, too, that their priorities, values, and purposes are being met, not just the therapist's.

Goals voiced at the start of treatment do not have to be ultimate ones. Any goal each partner or the therapist agrees upon is acceptable if it is plausible. As therapy continues, unexpected goals or related problems that must be dealt with may come to the fore. The therapist has to help the couple separate valid goals from those that are distractions or indicate resistance. Progressing stepwise is theoretically ideal, but that is often interrupted by life's immediate necessities.

Clients often define their goals at first in terms of their present complaints: "We're always fighting. If only he wouldn't jump on me all the time, we would be okay." Or "I feel that she no longer loves me. I can't get overtime work any more and so money is tight. The minute I come in the door now, she wants me to fix things. She doesn't think about me." Or a third: "I have trouble with sex, that is, in keeping my erection, and I never used to until these past six months when she found out I had a one-night stand." And a fourth: "I'm stuck here with this house, the kids, and a station wagon. He's never home. He's married more to that company than to me."

It would be simplistic to believe that each situation could be easily remedied: in the first case, if one instructed the woman's husband to stop jumping on her; in the second, if the man made more money and his wife gave him time to relax; in the third, if the man were relieved of guilt about his sexual experience and his wife would "forgive" him; and in the fourth case, if the husband were urged to spend more time with his family and give more directly of himself. Of course, no such simple solutions exist.

All these complaints are derivative of other problems. Obviously much more is involved in each instance than can be significantly changed by a commonsense suggestion. If it could be done that easily it would have been, and professional help would not have been sought.

More sophisticated couples may state their immediate goals differently, but these, too, often emerge from derivative complaints. More subtle versions of the previous examples might be: "My wife and I don't communicate meaningfully any more—we can talk about things, but not feelings." Or "Yes, I can write checks, too, but we really don't have equal responsibility or rights when it comes to making decisions about significant expenditures. He can decide to buy a new suit for himself, but if I want a coat I have to ask him if it's okay to spend the money now." The presumed goals in response to these two complaints would be to "improve communication" in the first instance, and to arrive at a suitable modus operandi for money management in the second. In pursuing these two goals, we shortly discover how derivative these complaints are. The first, that of poor communication, may be a manifestation of the wife's need to maintain distance. In the second example, the use of money may be but one among many manifestations of these mates' deep struggle for power.

The therapist's first challenge is to help the couple establish what they really want. This is often best defined in behavioral terms even when insight is also required to produce change. It may be important for partners to learn that the overt expression of their complaints is rooted in fundamental differences that must be acknowledged if the power struggle is to become less crucial in their daily interactions. Or the therapist may elect to bypass the immediate problem and help them work more directly on power, returning to, say, money conflicts later if the spouses have not resolved those problems themselves by then. When covenants are used to clarify the underlying sources that produce disputes, appropriate immediate goals become clearer.

When the therapist and clients are reasonably sure that both mates, even if ambivalent, really wish to try to improve their relationship, they may then proceed, on a step-by-step basis, to set goals. Some couples are satisfied with traveling a short distance down the road to their ideal of the perfect relationship; others want to make leaps—they are too impatient to rest for long at intermediate points.

In either case, goals must be attainable to be effective. It is the therapist's duty not to accept impossible or destructive goals, such as "I want my wife to obey me" or "Ours must be a perfect relationship without arguments or fights." The therapist must not allow a common goal to be set if one of the partners cannot possibly fulfill it or does not wish to accept it.

A nonacceptable goal appeared in one marriage in which the husband was subject to depression and fits of uncontrollable rage, triggered by incidents that appeared to lack clear causes. Although already middle-aged and in a profession in which he was well recognized, he had a secret ambition to become President of the United States. His wife supported his ambition semihumorously, but underneath she too was serious. They were in a borderline *folie à deux* that embarrassed them and yet was very real to them. At expense to the man's professional work and to the couple's family life, they became active in local politics. His underlying goal originally was for me to help him change his personality so that he could better achieve his ambition to become president. The wife was more for the goal of eliminating her husband's irrational rages and depressions, which were usually directed against her.

After he agreed to work with his wife and me on the more immediate goal of dealing with his depression and rage, we postponed discussing his presidential goal and dealt with his not fulfilling his wife's covenant regarding his behavior to her.

The symptoms of depression and rage were connected with the fact that when the man was young he had seen his father as an absolute monarch; both at home and in business, his slightest desire was carried out by those around him, particularly his wife. The boy perceived everyone as adoring and admiring his wise and powerful father. Now, as a man, his covenant was to be adored and for his word to be law, as his father's had been. His wife did not always act in the prescribed fashion. He viewed himself as inadequate compared to his father, while, at the same time, he fancied he was omnipotent. His depression and rage occurred whenever some event impinged to demonstrate that he was not really as powerful as he was in fantasy.

The husband's presidential goal came to the forefront again later on, when it could be dealt with better. It was clear that his ambitions had continued to lurk in the background, but to have tried to deal directly with this goal at the beginning of treatment could have created the dilemma Dr. Robert Lindner described, in his case history "The Jet-Propelled Couch" (from *The Fifty-Minute Hour*). Lindner entered his young patient's jet-sped delusion and became so deeply involved he made the delusion his own. He failed to perceive the point at which his patient no longer needed the delusion and discarded it, leaving Lindner still riding on the "jet-propelled couch."

It is not uncommon for a therapist to engage in a *folie à deux* with a patient. Lindner bravely offered his classic example as an appropriate clinical warning. In couple therapy, countertransference can also lead the therapist into joining a delusional or paranoid system of one mate against the other. I could not accept my client's goal to help him change his personality so that he could become president, but after some preliminary exploration that revealed the extent of this need, I asked him to put off our dealing with it, hoping that he would discard the ambition of his own accord. Ordinarily, I might have pointed out his illogical position to him, but I sensed that it would be unwise to do so here because of the emphasis he had put on his father as a godlike person whom he could never equal unless he achieved great political power. My pointing out the lack of logic in his ambition at that time could have made him see me as allied with his father to keep him in an inferior position.

If I had dwelt on the inappropriateness of his ambition I would have confirmed the "you are like my father who is so superior to me and compared to whom I will always be a boy" feelings he soon developed anyway. In part, his telling me his secret ambition had been a maneuver to get me to respond to him as he felt his father had. It was sometime later that I came to understand why a warning bell had rung in my ear when he told me his presidential ambition in the first session; it was too big a secret to tell so soon.

Goal-setting is a basic technique that implements certain important theories: (1) It enlists the couple and the therapist in working together for a purpose. (2) Goals motivate people and enlist their thinking ability as well as emotions in the therapeutic process. (3) It is a step toward maturation to be responsible for consciously establishing one's own goals, and to move toward achieving them in a conflict-free way. (4) Failure to be able to work toward reasonable goals implies a priori evidence that a basic negative factor exists in a marital system or subsystem. (5) It is the therapist's job to help a couple circumvent, or remove, their own roadblocks, when they do genuinely want to achieve their goals.

Tasks

Tasks that are designed to achieve goals must incorporate a couple's dynamics as well as the needs and psychodynamics of each partner. Tasks should teach and facilitate change through experience, but not kindle so much anxiety or resentment that they are rejected (unless a plan embraces rejecting a task for predictable therapeutic purposes). By making clear the problem areas and the underlying dynamics, covenants greatly facilitate devising suitable tasks. In fact, covenants serve as a guide for setting tasks that will change behavior or probe areas of resistance, and help partners fulfill each other's unconscious needs.

For example, the pleasuring exercises of sex therapy can be used as therapeutic tests in marital therapy. These explore a couple's capacity to accept closeness, to collaborate, to give and receive, to communicate, and to accept directions from each other without feeling put down.

Tasks may be for one mate alone, or for both together, or they may involve each doing something for the other. They are carried out at home and all are designed to produce behavioral changes; some are expected to yield insight, some are not. An example of an insight-producing task is a paradoxical one that makes behavior that is acceptable to a client *un*acceptable. This usually entails having a mate carry out to an absurd extent a behavioral pattern that is disturbing to the partner.

For example, a wife complained that her husband was untidy at home, and he confirmed this. The wife tried unsuccessfully to change her husband's ways, alternately yelling at him and picking up after him, much as his mother had done. The man was instructed to be as slovenly as he could possibly be—really to mess things up; at the same time, the woman was instructed to keep berating him angrily but *not* to clean up after him. Even if she did not feel inclined to do so, she was to shout at him if he left anything carelessly about the house. Each spouse heard the instructions to the other in the session. (The therapist must give such instructions with a straight face and must convincingly convey that he really does want his instructions to be followed.)

When carried to such a ridiculous extent, the behavior of each partner becomes clear to the other; insight into the effects of one's own behavior is almost immediate, and frequently both change their behavior of their own accord. In this case, the husband realized sheepishly that he was acting like a spoiled brat and the wife saw herself as the proverbial shrew. Both laughed ruefully at what had happened. Each realized that the exaggeration of their usual behavior was alien to their egos. By means of this simple task we had changed behavior that each had considered acceptable to the reverse; both spouses altered their irritating actions.

In the conjoint session following a task assignment, the spouses describe what they did and their reactions to it. A therapist is concerned with how the assignments were carried out and what the spouses felt. What was good about it, what was not? How did each cope with the other's task as well as his own? Failure—why a task was not carried out—is as important to learn about as is success. Failures, resistance, and emotional reactions form the grist for a therapeutic session. Dealing with these requires all of a professional's skill, his technical and theoretical knowledge in coping with immediate as well as remote causes.

A fascinating challenge for the therapist is to develop tasks that will tap the unconscious desires and needs of each partner. The therapist has to assay rapidly the unconscious terms of the covenants so that they can serve as a guide. This was done, for example, in the Anderson case, when each of these childlike partners was trying to make the other a strong but benevolent and giving parent. Each partner's need to be both dependent and in charge was dealt with by putting each in charge of family decisions for alternating periods of three days, so that the conflict over who was in charge and how to appear to abdicate control while making the other mate act as one wanted was solved. Each began to feel safe when it was the other's turn to be in charge and neither did anything detrimental to the other. A feeling of trust slowly developed.

Problems that originate primarily in the first and second contract categories—expectations of marriage and biological as well as intrapsychic factors—can frequently be met through tasks, combined with techniques of brief psychotherapy. These are used to bypass or work through the sources of reactions and feelings that are then brought to light in the following session.

With a professional's bag of tricks at your disposal, and the considerable knowledge you have gained about yourself by now, you should be ready to do a good job on your own couple covenant.

When Negotiations Break Down

Although most couples who commit themselves to working out a couple covenant are successful even beyond their expectations, some fail. While it is relatively easy to think out their *private* covenants, some couples—or some individuals —cannot go beyond that by themselves.

There are several reasons why it may be harder for them than for others to work toward a couple covenant. Some partners become so angry that it is impossible for them to talk about anything without weeping, withdrawing, shouting, or becoming abusive. Others become intolerably anxious. One man confessed that he was sure his partner would leave him if he exposed his expectations and she learned what he was really like. Of course, she *did* know what he was like—but he did not know that. He sincerely believed that she (and everyone else) perceived him as strong, competent, and reliable, although he was none of those things. In fact, he fooled no one but himself, and that was enough to keep him from cooperating with his partner.

Some people are more afraid of hearing what is in their mate's covenant than they are of revealing their own. Those with low self-esteem expect to hear only that they are total failures in every respect, and they may lack the courage to face the imagined crushing blows to which they will be subjected.

The major roadblock to working out a covenant is the fear of change. We have all known times when we felt safer staying with what was familiar—even if it wasn't much good—than venturing into the unknown. When Hamlet in his soliloquy says that we would rather bear those ills we have than fly to others that we know not of, he is speaking of another matter, but he could well be referring to commonplace resistance to personal change.

Whenever we want to improve a relationship, to give more in order to get more, we have to alter our actions. And that is not easy. Merely making a resolution to change one's behavior is no more likely to be successful than making a New Year's resolution to stop smoking or start exercising. In order to change, we have to be *ready* —and motivated—to do so. If your relationship is a fairly good one, you may not want to change it—because essentially it is not bad enough to be worth the effort. If your relationship is not very good, you may still think that keeping the status quo is easier than doing anything about it—but that is because you may not have given much thought about what is going to happen ultimately. Generally speaking, living situations rarely remain static for long; if things do not get better, they tend to get worse.

If, when you try to work on your couple covenant, you find that you fight, become depressed, anxious, fearful—or just feel it is too much trouble—perhaps this is something you cannot do alone; you may need the help of a therapist. Couple therapy, individual sessions, or a combination of the two might get you started. Many couples who seek therapy find themselves immeasurably happier, and their lives greatly enriched, as a result. The couple covenant can be used to great advantage in conjunction with all psychological forms of therapy. Since the covenant is a concept, not a psychological or inter-personal test, any therapist can adapt the concept to his or her needs as well as to those of the couple. In this way, therapist and clients can remain free to move around within the framework of their own requirements. And of course, different couples do have different needs. When two people want to remain together because they are bound by (not simply need) strength, affection, and love, the therapist has the best of all situations to work with; the only limits are his or her own perceptiveness and ingenuity.

But not all couples *do* want to remain together, and some who want to should not if the goals of their two private covenants are in direct conflict with those of their couple system. The O'Dwyers were such a case.

Leona and Jerry had been living together for two years when Leona announced that she wasn't getting any younger and thought it was time to get married and have a child. Jerry argued that they had a good thing and asked "Why change a winning game?" so many times that Leona threatened to walk out forever if he did it once more. Jerry wasn't particularly interested in having children, and he certainly didn't feel ready to marry. But he understood Leona's sense of urgency and knew that unless he went along with her he would lose her. It was a difficult decision to make but, in the end, Jerry decided to "sacrifice his freedom" and take the plunge. Although the O'Dwyers' lifestyle was substantially the same after the wedding as it had been for the preceding two years, Jerry felt hopelessly trapped and resentful; the marriage was in trouble from the beginning.

If the O'Dwyers had known about covenants, Jerry might have discovered that for everything he gave up when he married he stood to gain something valuable in return; instead of lamenting his imaginary losses, he might have been trying to make his marriage work. But Jerry was doing just the opposite: he seemed to look for situations that enabled him to say "We had a winning game and we changed it, so now we have a losing game. You got what you wanted and I hope you're happy!" This speech was usually his cue to slam the door and go down to the local bar for a night of morose drinking.

There are many transactions that set off predictable reactions even though the partners, in trying to reconstruct the event, find it hard to see what made things go wrong. The triggering incidents are often so subtle they escape notice; the origins of these set patterns are lost in the couple's ancient history. It is fruitless to try to figure out who did what to whom first, although many people do try, and display great glee each time they think they have scored a point.

Transactions that have become set patterns, and the feelings they arouse, can be changed by a number of methods—but seldom can that be done easily by amateurs. Usually professional assistance is required.

Often, by the time a couple arrives in a therapist's office, one or both may have decided on separation as a goal. If the situation is clearly beyond hope—that is, if at least one has made an irrevocable decision—it is the therapist's job to help the partners separate with as little destructiveness as possible. But the therapist should proceed cautiously, because some couples seem unable to get along at all until they are threatened with separation. One or both of the partners may be using the threat to try to improve the relationship or to force them both to seek professional help.

Therapists try to help couples continue their relationships if the couples want to. For a therapist to decide unilaterally that a couple should divorce, or to urge this on them against their own inclinations, is to play God. If a couple or one mate is determined to separate, they should be helped to realize that the separation of two people who once loved each other is always a bitter disappointment as well as a blow to each one's self-esteem. It is the end of a hope, a dream, and a relationship that may have been beautiful at one time—and it is painful to accept.

If a couple has children, they should know that the children and their relationships with them may be deeply affected. They should know, too, that parents can do a great deal to minimize potential injury to their children if they make a careful and informed effort.

Those who separate should know also that they are likely to meet economic hardship. At the very least, if they decide to separate, the couple should understand *why* they are doing it, what went wrong, and what remained right. Everything they can learn from the experience they had together will enhance their chances for greater self-fulfillment and for a better relationship next time.

It is up to the therapist to provide enough firm leadership to establish without any doubt whether or not both partners want to stay together and improve their relationship. If they are not sure, they should clarify their covenants in the course of therapy and find out what it is they really want so that they can make a wise decision.

If, after thorough investigation, the partners realize that they neither give nor get what they want from each other, the decision to separate is usually a positive one and should be seen as such. Measuring the value of therapy by the number of marriages it "saves" is invalid. It is *people* who need to be saved, not a relationship that cannot be loving or fruitful.

Sometimes a request for therapeutic help is a fraud; one or both partners may turn up in a therapist's office with covert goals. For example, a woman whose husband is given to depression and is very dependent on her may have made up her mind to leave him but be worried that he will go into a severe depression or a psychotic break; she is terrified that he will commit suicide. But if she can leave him in the protective hands of a therapist, she thinks she will be relieved of guilt, because it is not as if she "just walked out and left him to cope on his own"; someone else will be "responsible."

Similarly, a man who is soon to depart might fear the tremendous rage his wife will let loose on him when he breaks the news. He will enter couple therapy with her so that the therapist will be a party to the announcement and share the responsibility; the presence of a third person will also provide him with a certain amount of protection, he believes.

Some mates go through the motions of therapy so that they can later tell themselves, each other, their children, friends, relatives, and even God that they "tried everything there was to try before making the decision."

Even when the decision has been made, it is a good idea not to rush. Just as courtship should take a certain amount of time, so should separation. It takes a significant number of months to work out the emotional and mechanical aspects of separation and to prepare to live without a partner.

Although the vast majority of people can live without a mate, most of those who have been in a close relationship for some period of time are not at all sure that they can. It is important for them to learn that they *are* able to survive, to live alone, and to take care of themselves. If they really believe it, it will prevent their clutching at the first warm body that comes along out of fear of loneliness or helplessness. Then, when a suitable partner does appear, they can join each other knowing that they have really chosen, not fallen together because they are afraid of being alone.

Any couple unable to maintain a good relationship needs to know that each might be able to do so with a different partner. You remember that each behavioral profile was of an individual *in a given relationship;* the interaction of two people is always more important than the psychodynamics of one person alone. It is sometimes astonishing to see how people leave desperately unhappy arrangements and manage to find someone whose needs beautifully complement their own.

During the early years of their marriage Fran and Victor Goldberg worked hard together and were happy together. With a small inheritance Victor bought a run-down candle-making plant and strove to turn it into a successful business. Fran became assistant-of-all-work in the factory office; she answered the telephone, kept the books, handled the correspondence and the payroll. In addition, she contributed a number of ideas for novelty candles and Victor, unable to afford a designer, was happy to discover that she was so creative.

Over the years the business flourished and so did the Goldbergs. They had good sex, enjoyed each other's company, loved one another, and, through the business, were engaged in a common cause. They eventually had three children, and after the first one was born Fran began to stay at home. By this time the business had grown: Victor had expanded the building, maintained an office staff of four, and taken on a full-time creative director. Now the head of a lucrative business, Victor proved an excellent executive.

The Goldbergs had recently bought a house in a fine suburb, they sent their children to the "best schools," and Fran had virtually anything she wanted. But she was not happy. She frequently complained that as Victor became more successful he had become more and more removed from their life together. He gave her money and *things,* she said, but he no longer gave her love.

She felt, too, that she was nothing but another suburban house-wife, chauffeuring children, playing tennis, and going to PTA and committee meetings. She claimed she hated every minute of it, was bored and stifled—yet she made no move to go back to school, look for an interesting job, or develop any of her own interests.

Victor was unsympathetic to her complaints because, with the good housekeeper they employed, Fran was free to do whatever she wanted to do. The only reason she didn't do anything, he began to believe, was that she was envious of his success in the business with-out her and therefore devoted herself to making him miserable to get back at him. He accused her of failing to appreciate his hard work and many accomplishments. She would like it better, he said, if she could turn back the clock to the time when they were poor but equal as they worked side by side.

Fran and Victor were both right. In their unhappiness, each of them had even had a few extramarital experiences to prove that they could "get more affection from a stranger than I can from you," although neither had developed any deep involvement with anyone else.

Fran believed that the man she had loved and married had become materialistic, unloving, emotionally ungiving. Victor believed that he was neither appreciated nor loved, that his wife looked only for opportunities to belittle him in public and in private. Neither could be supportive of the other any more and neither cared to com-municate. Each was preoccupied with trying to substantiate her or his own position. Each wanted love, but insisted that the other must be the first to change.

After a period of therapy, the Goldbergs arrived at a mutual decision to divorce. They stayed together only long enough to work out an amicable property, child-support, and alimony agreement.

On her first vacation as a single woman, Fran met a man on an airplane and married him a year later. Victor didn't take as long; he was remarried within eight months of the divorce. His new wife admires him for his position in business as well as for his personal attributes; she loves him dearly, protects him from others, and sup-ports him where and when he needs it; he reciprocates in every way.

The same is true of Fran and her new husband. They are mutually loving, admiring, and supportive. The Goldbergs were lucky to find new partners so quickly to give them the love and acceptance they wanted—and to fulfill the other requirements they could not meet for each other.

That happy ending took place twelve years ago. Both remarried couples are as content today as they were then.

Not all divorces lead to such a delightful outcome for both partners; even so, the Goldbergs were wise to end a relationship in which neither could respond to the other's needs and in which hatred and paranoia had set the tone for their household. In their new choices, each found a good complementary relationship. Each was surprised that the other could do so.

This case is not unusual; certain conflicts cannot be dealt with in a creative fashion. When two private covenants are in such opposition that they are serious sources of anxiety, either or both partners are likely to conclude that the relationship is untenable. They often decide to go their separate ways—and often they should, but not without exploring their situation with a skilled therapist first.

If the main conflict is due to neurotic factors in one or both mates, couple therapy may or may not prove workable; in some cases a period of individual therapy is helpful, with a return to conjoint therapy later on. It is difficult to reconcile conflicts when they are stubborn manifestations of opposing inner needs, when either partner is emotionally ill, or when a significant difference exists in the intelligence of the two partners.

One formidable problem is a lack of sexual attraction. Another crops up if one partner is terribly anxious most of the time and neither is able—or wants—to relieve the anxiety. This often emerges when one is a "clinging vine" and the other cannot begin to deal with so much dependence or the anxiety it creates. The more independent partner may be completely insensitive to the clinging one's needs. Or, he or she may be aware of the dependency and feel helpless in the face of it, rendered anxious in turn, and then act in a destructive way. The more constructive course is to be a sympathetic listener and a supportive partner but, at the same time, to urge the anxious person to seek professional help. The clinging vine is unlikely to change without outside assistance.

Every once in a while a therapist encounters a couple who both cling—who, as the cliché goes, can't live with each other and can't live without each other. The Millers were a case in point.

When they came for treatment, David was fifty-four, Pamela forty-one; they had been married for eighteen years and had lived separately for nine of them, although they had never stopped seeing each other socially. There were two children, a girl who was then sixteen and a boy of fourteen. The Millers reported that they had poor sex because David was impotent with Pamela and avoided her sexually for that reason.

David was handsome, verbal, polished—a worldly gentleman. Pam was beautiful, intelligent, and also verbal. She appeared to be more anxious than David but, like him, had great poise and charm.

Since Pam is thirteen years David's junior, at the time of their marriage she felt unsophisticated, childlike, and ill-fitted to move into his circle of friends. They had had fine sex before they were married and for three years afterward, during which period David was warm and affectionate. But beginning with the fourth year, he grew increasingly hostile and, more and more often, impotent. Pam felt rejected by his impotence, and each time it occurred it made her weep—and that made David furious.

After six years of marriage the Millers decided to separate. David then revealed that for the last three years he had had a crush on a younger woman, with whom he had excellent sex. Although David moved out at that time, the pair did not try for a legal separation and stayed in constant touch. They saw each other from time to time, called each other frequently to talk over matters having to do with their children, family social activities, and so on. They continued to file joint tax returns. David met all his financial obligations promptly and cheerfully and kept a close, warm relationship with his children.

The separation lasted three years. Then Pam told David she was considering remarriage and wanted a divorce. David came home at once to "tell her off and arrange for the divorce," but instead, he moved in and stayed. Pam was glad to have him back. For a little while they even had good sex together, but soon David began to be impotent again and to find fault constantly with Pam.

Fortunately for her, she had learned during the separation that she did not have to be completely dependent on David, so she was able to manage when, after three years of reconciliation, he again left her for another, younger woman with whom he ostensibly functioned well sexually.

That was six years ago. After that David visited his family regularly and stayed with them occasionally. He and Pam continued to appear together at various social functions although each of them was dating others. Pam had no sexual problems with other men.

Finally she insisted on professional help. She told David, "It's time to work this out. Either we stay together and make it—sexually and every other way—or we get a divorce and get it over with once and for all." Her sudden demand for action followed David's spending a weekend with close mutual friends and taking along another woman. Pam was both angry and insulted by this; she said that although she went out with other men she did it discreetly and didn't flaunt her dates with people they both knew.

David was willing to go with her to the therapist's office. He wasn't sure how he felt about her at the time. He knew that originally he had felt protective of her, but didn't any longer. On the other hand, she was a bright and attractive companion and he felt that her presence enhanced his prestige. He questioned his ability to love anyone; he was preoccupied (as was Pam) with appearance, form, and style.

Unlike David, Pam was quite definite about her feelings. She said that she still loved David but could no longer tolerate her unsettled status. She kept insisting that he decide either to make things work or get out of her life.

But David could not be pushed into a decision. He saw no reason to get a divorce and, as time went on, it became clear that he did not want to change anything at all. The status quo suited him perfectly—except that he did wish Pam would go back to school, finish her degree, and begin to share the financial burden.

The therapeutic plan was to explore the Millers' covenants with them as soon as possible in order to determine whether or not they saw reasons to break the bond that held them "half together." It is always important for a therapist to respect the needs that have kept two individuals locked into what appears an impossible situation. Some systems should not be tampered with unless at least one partner really wants a change. Did either Pam or David want to make a complete break, or could both accept living together again? They were both open and in touch with their feelings, and they talked about themselves with great ease. Although each had had several years of psychoanalysis, they agreed that it had not improved them as a team.

When the Millers wrote out their individual covenants, they were instructed to do so according to the three levels of consciousness rather than the three categories. David prefaced his with the statement "I have the impression that I have to find the solutions in the third level—Beyond Awareness—before I can find any in the other two."

DAVID'S COVENANT

Levels I. and II.   Conscious, Verbalized and Not Verbalized

What I Want—and/or Get

1. I expect you to keep me sexually interested and active. I need that form of ego reassurance—perhaps to ward off some faint, lingering misgivings about my masculinity. Whenever I can arouse a woman I am rewarded sexually and psychically.

2. I don't want you to be overdependent. I do want you to make your own way, make money. I won't last forever and my high earnings won't, either.

3. I don't want you to betray me. But maybe I don't really mean that. I become intensely and even irrationally involved with you when I feel threatened by your infidelity; I have a neurotic need—

not unpleasant—to feel slightly endangered by your actions with other men.

4. I want you to be my child. Pay attention. Learn. Respect my gray hairs. But notice that I'm really youthful, attractive to women of all ages—although I much prefer the younger ones.

5. You've done a good job with the kids, but you've been over-protective. It's good to see you loosen up a bit, even if it has been only for your convenience. You *have* borne the brunt of the job of putting in the time to care for them—less than you claim, but lots, nonetheless.

What I'm Willing to Give

All I can offer is a show of marital attention. You don't turn me on. But I'm pleasant to guests (unless we squabble), personable, bright. I can't give you love in any dramatic—or perhaps even real —sense. I get crushes, usually related to sex, and can be fond of people. But I don't *love* anyone. Maybe only myself? I'll philander— unless some miracle occurs between us. And maybe even then.

Level III.   Beyond Awareness

It's not so easy to figure out what's in my unconscious, but I know this much: it's something in my unconscious that makes me fear you and other women. With a new, young lover, I'm in charge, worshiped. Invariably, they all learn (as you did) my weaknesses; then I'm afraid of being controlled and I become impotent and must back off. I actually do become frightened that you will control me. I know it relates to my mother—I learned that much in five years of analysis—but all that analysis hasn't changed it. And I don't want any more prolonged treatment. If I haven't changed by now, I won't.

PAM'S COVENANT

Level I.   Conscious: Verbalized

What I Want/Get

1. I have a sense of equality now. But I didn't at the start. I wanted you to be my teacher. You were.

2. You give me prestige which I enjoy and profit by.

3. We share friends, interests, children, achievements, pleasures, and many common goals. We work well together in many areas—we are an "attractive couple," and so forth. We enhance each other publicly; we help each other in this way.

What I'm Willing to Do/Give

1. My enthusiastic and rather joyful temperament, which is beneficial to you. I first became aware of it on our honeymoon. I enjoy this part of me, so it isn't hard to give.

Level II.   Conscious but Not Verbalized

What I Want/Get

1. I'm insecure and anxious in social situations; I depend on you for initial entrees to people who intimidate me (people more powerful than I am, the "grownups"). I need your nerve—your self-starting ability. At first I feel I'll be rejected—a hangover from my childhood of feeling insecure.

2. I'm afraid that you will compare me to others in this respect and I'll suffer by the comparison—to some of your lady friends. I'm very insecure because of this—I fear that you'll reject me because I'm not good enough. Although this has changed recently. And I know that you are insecure about your place with these people, too, and you need me. But I want your approval.

What I Give

1. In exchange for your protection and social support I give you support by my general attractiveness and the like. I also make you appear sexually adequate.

Level III.   Beyond Awareness

1. I am nothing without you. I need you and I love you for that because it means that you're so much better than I. I need you like a father protector.

2. Because I need you like a father I'm depressed sexually. I hate you and love you for this. You won't give to me sexually. In one way, you are close to the childish part of me, and you are apart from me in the adult fashion. You need me so much—you'll never love anyone else. I want you as a father; my "teach-me" syndrome.

3. I want you as a lover. I have a sense of extreme deprivation about this—but I'm afraid of it, too.

4. I want closeness.

5. I don't want closeness, because of my father hangups.

6. I won't measure up sexually to your other women.

7. I know I can make relationships with other men—stronger, more powerful, richer, and sexually able. I will if I have to. But I want *you*. Because you aren't available?

8. Our relationship is sadomasochistic. The games we play out, money, decisions, competition between us, your constantly putting me down. You want me to be humbled, a child. Does this still excite me?

9. I am able to frighten you, and I do it consciously. I now know my strengths and your weaknesses. I know you are afraid to have sex with me. I want it. I'll help you.

The Millers' covenants expose the core of their relationship; they are both aware of what they do, but not while they are doing it. They have been unable to change.

This couple's position is seen professionally by C.J.S. as follows:

Theirs is a very deep sadomasochistic relationship. They started out eighteen or so years ago with David as a powerful parental partner and Pamela as a childlike one. They now take turns reversing these roles in their interactional cycle. One of them says or does something and then the roles switch. He becomes the child and perceives her as a controlling mother; she then behaves in a way that is threatening to him. As soon as he is ahead with her, he feels frightened and gives up control, thrusting it on Pam. When she has it (and uses it) he then becomes angry and frightened, sees her as his captor. He does a very neat job on himself as she falls into her role assignment. Aspects of this game continue, although he is now less of a father image for her.

Pam has become an accomplished woman; she wants to be a romantic child partner, but with a man who is powerful and will also be a good father, not the punitive one as David is. (Or does she? Up to now she has not developed a significant relationship with another man.) David's threat, and the reality of his having left home, play into the fact that her father did disappear when she was three. David's reappearance reinforces the fantasy that Daddy will come back. But soon after he returns she is glad to have him leave again because he is so hostile.

The emotional impact of David's ways is lessened somewhat for her by now, because the constant awakening of her warm and hopeful feelings, followed inevitably by disappointment, has begun to desensitize her to her expectations. Rather than feeling intermittent positive reinforcement to her optimism whenever he comes home again, she reacts now more in response to a repetition-compulsion (i.e., by repeating a disturbing situation she learns to deal with it better and to find it less upsetting. If this is true it may mean that Pam *is* ready for change).

David depends on Pam to give credence to his masculinity, just as his handsome and urbane presence reinforces her public image of femininity. Meanwhile, he is free to try to reinforce his self-image and defiantly show his independence of Pam through affairs with young, beautiful women with whom he is sexually competent—until he feels he has conquered each, and he loses his superiority mystique with them. At that point he makes the woman into a mother and becomes impotent. He feels the woman "will stomp on me with iron boots" (a fascinating and at the same time frightening prospect to him—his masochism loves it; his defensive sadism makes him act first by attacking). Flight, distance—both physically and emotionally—are his defenses. Pam now recognizes that she is "too strong" for him. She knows now that she has power, except that she cannot control his flight and impotence, both of which infuriate her. She stated that she lost her love for him when she realized he could no longer play the role of strong protector and teacher for her. David's covenant in some respects was more to the point about where they are now. Pam's was addressed to the past and did not fully convey her current feelings.

I asked them to arrange to spend a night together without the children. This suddenly became a great logistical problem despite the fact that they had two apartments. I asked them, as a task assignment, to pleasure one another's bodies without touching the genitals. As I gave them the instructions, David repeatedly said that Pam did not turn him on, that he was a philanderer and couldn't love. I heard his message and explained the sensual and communicative aspects of the exercise; it was not to be sexual, there was to be no coitus or attempt to give each other an orgasm.

Their sadomasochistic picture was clear from the covenants. Whoever is in control must hurt the other; the pleasuring exercise made this clearly apparent as we progressed.

The first home session of pleasuring without genital touch. Pam was anxious. The day they were to see each other she "had an impulse to go to a lawyer and get it over with." She went home, rearranged books, and did needless tasks to master her anxiety. When David came in, he too was anxious. He was not looking forward to the experience, even though I had stressed that they were not to have coitus. He questioned Pam's desire to go through with it. Assured that she wanted to, he then assumed the parental role, tried to put her at ease, and quickly moved them to the bedroom.

When they got into bed, Dave immediately stated that he did not plan to stay all night. (This cue put their negative interactional script into operation at once.) Pam let him know that she felt rejected. He then tried to woo her but he felt annoyed at her feeling rejected. They relaxed, hugged, talked, stroked each other's bodies to some extent—they enjoyed the talk most. After an hour Dave left. Pam cried for a short time and then stopped, feeling she was silly to have expected more from him.

The second pleasuring session, one week later (*with genital touch, but no coitus, no orgasm*). These instructions were designed to remove the pressure of having to perform.

They spent a weekend in her apartment but avoided pleasuring each other because the children were there, although her bedroom offered adequate privacy. Pam pointed out in the following conjoint session that she pulls back when he distances himself this way because she so fears his rejection. He says he feels that he had better not come close to her or he will be stomped on "with those iron boots." They therefore slept in separate rooms and did nothing sensual that weekend. He used the children to avoid any intimate contact with Pam.

The next weekend. Pam arranged for the children to be away. David felt ill at ease with his protectors gone. When they went to bed he pleasured Pam, but because she felt he was hurried she did not enjoy it. She said it took the heart out of her, so that she was not with it when it came to pleasuring him. (This encapsulates their relationship.)

Their script.

PAM: I anticipate that he will reject me and of course he does. I feel angry at him for this.

DAVE: Pam is angry at me. She [as his mother] will stomp on me. I am frightened. I do not care to give her anything.

In the session in which they described their weekend they each brought out their feelings and reactions openly. Communication was good, but it did not have the effect of lessening the anger or anxiety of either. Instead they both used it to confirm that each had reason to be upset with the other.

The third pleasuring, one week later (*same instructions*). They were at my office the next morning, so the events were fresh in their memories.

DAVE: I am tense in these things [the pleasuring].

PAM: Just your body is there—not this part [she holds his hand tenderly].

DAVE (to me): We started to touch—but I got more controlled. Pam touched me—including my penis—and *nothing came of it* [said emphatically and with pathos—as the final proof of their (his) hopelessness]. Pam then got sleepy when she did it to me.

PAM: When he did it to me I got excited this time—but when I did it to him he was so distant *I went away further by falling asleep.*

Dave then went on to say that the pleasuring and touching make him tense, that he knows he can't respond—isn't this sufficient proof that their relationship is no good? Pam said she was willing to go away if he no longer wanted her. I stated that David's feelings had to be respected and that this did seem to confirm that they might as well divorce. As soon as I mentioned divorce they both said that they wanted to continue treatment.

The fourth evening together (*pleasuring again*). Both felt better because somehow they felt "no need to perform, no gymnastics." It was pleasant for both. (My confrontation of them in the previous session had caused them to draw a little closer together; they had consolidated against the enemy, who was challenging the status quo they had demanded that I challenge.) They were friendlier to each other. He was straightforward and said that an evening like that just helped him to stall. He had finally realized he did not have to perform and therefore felt fine. He had not had an erection, he said pointedly, in case Pam and I misunderstood his message. I then asked them, "What would you like to do the next evening together?"

DAVID: I get an immediate association to a Sartre character. I could cut off my own penis as an existential act. [That said it all! I felt great empathy but I also realized that they had to play out the rest of their script their own way.] He then smiled and said he and Pam had planned that they would play that she would be his date and come to his apartment next week.

The fifth evening, one week later. They went to the theater and then to his apartment—both opting to act as new dates and not to refer to their long history together. They spent the night together.

David said he had had no sexual response to Pam. Pam said she felt rejected and depressed. As he pleasured her, she had fantasized herself at an attorney's office making divorce arrangements. She had realized, as David changed to masturbating her, that he had not kissed her during these past several weeks. She wondered why he avoided this intimacy. She became aware *at that point* that she had become aroused quickly, and as David continued to masturbate her she had an orgasm.

David then stated matter-of-factly that he usually got excited when he turned a woman on—but not with Pam (a devastating put-down that was meant to hurt, yet conversely it was her fantasy of hurting him by seeing the lawyer, plus her injured feeling at the realization he had not kissed her, that made her excited and led to her climax). I pointed out how important it was for each to hurt the other—neither dared to risk a sustained campaign of staying in close. I asked what I thought was a rhetorical question: "Why take turns chasing after each other when you both know you are unattainable to the other?" David said (although no response was expected) that both of them liked to be kicked; Pam answered, "I am bored by simple men and bored by men who adore me."

I told them I did not know how to help them to change. They did not seem to want either to come closer, or to divorce; both of them seemed to want the situation as it was. David immediately said they should stop treatment. Pam acquiesced. So did I.

They left treatment. I doubted that any change had taken place.

When I sent them letters a year later David did not respond. Pamela replied that after their last session with me she had realized that she had no hope or desire for a reconciliation. She viewed David's readiness to leave therapy as justification for her decision. For her all conflicts and anxieties stemming from their difficulties had disappeared; she felt freed. She told me they had now taken legal steps to dissolve their marriage but I wondered if they would ever complete a legal divorce.

The Millers' story has been told here as an extreme example of negotiations that break down and stay broken down. This kind of interaction is not common—but it is not rare, either. The case is intended to serve as a reminder that only those who are *willing* to change, can. Because the Millers were not, they did not. And possibly they never will.

The case is also illustrative of how resistant to change private covenants can be—for even though they worked in a negative way, the Millers' covenants were strong enough to defeat their couple system, the couple themselves, and their therapist as well.

10

Living up to the Covenant

If you and your partner have worked on a joint covenant, you have probably recognized by now that the *process* of doing the work was of more value to you than the document you wound up with. That is as it should be. The covenant *is* actually a process, not a "thing." For that reason, as you and your circumstances change from year to year, from month to month, even from minute to minute, you may have to make changes in your covenant.

We are all familiar with the weight-reducing precept that no diet works unless you change your eating habits: without this active change the dieter gains back all the lost pounds shortly after the diet is over. The couple covenant is dependent on the same kind of behavior modification—it is not a "deal" that you negotiate and have done with, once and for all, like a real estate contract. It is, instead, a way of living your life together, a mode of thinking, a new method of interacting. Changes in behavior often produce changes in feeling, too.

One of the major detriments to modern marriage is the notion that good relationships can change spontaneously, that if two people love each other everything will "work out." Surely it is no accident that our record-breaking divorce rate is highest among those who marry youngest, those most apt to believe that things will take care of themselves. The young are also more likely to have unrealistic expectations—to think that because they are married everything will always be perfect. But the young have no monopoly on this kind of fallacious thinking. Only the very wise, at any age, know that nothing is perfect and that all relationships need nurturing, and need it *all the time*. Living up to your covenant is the way to nurture your relationship.

Throughout the discussion of covenants we have talked about expectations. Everyone expects a relationship to be personally fulfilling; fulfillment is the only *purpose* of the relationship. When we speak of being happy or unhappy in a relationship or of having a good or bad marriage, we are saying that most of our expectations have or have not been fulfilled, that we are or are not frequently disappointed—or that our wants are mutual or contradictory.

But no one continues to keep the same expectations over the course of a lifetime, and as our expectations change, our perception of disappointment changes, too. There may have been various times in your life when you expected to be class president, to be satisfied with a salary of ten thousand dollars a year, to get a puppy for Christmas, or to be a professional basketball player. If you were disappointed in any of those aspirations, it may not matter any more because you have a completely different set of needs and dreams now.

These are simplistic analogies, but they illustrate how our expectations are changed by inner and outer forces: experiences (growing up, becoming older, or wiser), changing times, new people and influences in our lives.

In the first chapter of this book we discussed the widespread confusion we have all felt about our needs because of the changed and changing nature of male and female roles and of the function of marriage: marriage is no longer a system for physical survival and reproduction, but a means to emotional gratification.

In addition to this, a radical revision has gone on in marital life cycles—the various stages husbands and wives pass through together. At the middle of the last century, a typical married couple remained married for thirty-four years and the woman spent the entire time as a homemaker. She had six children, was thirty-six when the last was born, and almost fifty-nine when the last one married. Her husband had already died by that time and she herself died a couple of years later.

By contrast, a woman born in the mid-twentieth century is likely to have two children, the last born before she is thirty. She'll be little more than fifty-two when the last child marries (even younger when that child leaves home) and at least sixty-five before her husband dies. During the twentieth century alone, the so-called empty-nest period has become a major part of married life: after the last child marries, the couple still has at least thirteen years—nearly one-third or more of their forty-four-year marriage—alone together as a couple.

Nor is that all that is different. More than half of today's married women work outside the home, and more than one marriage in three ends in divorce.

In addition, couples used to go through a formal courting period, after which they married and settled into a life that consisted mainly of being parents. Of course they had needs and expectations that fluctuated, but their basic, major roles were almost always the same.

Today, most couples are likely to live together before marriage—the real start of their existence as a couple. Typically, the woman will have a job and will keep it until her first child is born. Once the children are in school (or even before), there is a strong likelihood that she will go back to work. She will have not one basic, major role as her predecessors did, but several different ones as an adult. As her roles change, so will her husband's, and the couple's needs and expectations will change with them.

In addition to these changes—during courtship, at marriage, after the birth of children, at the marriage of the children—there are other uncharted events that are bound to occur. These include major illnesses, moves, job changes, births, deaths, marriages and divorces among those who are close; accidents, disasters, varying financial positions—and any number of other possibilities. Every such event, major or minor, is likely to require some modification of the couple covenant.

Ideally, you would think in terms of your covenant as a firm way of life and make adjustments as you need to, almost automatically. But since we do not always operate according to ideals, you may want to reexamine your covenant at some point each year—perhaps the week following your anniversary (if you are married), on a birthday, the first day of spring, any time you are likely to remember. In addition, a renegotiation is in order any time you feel that your communication is not as good as it should be; if one or both of you seems to be unusually irritable, bored, or hostile; if either begins to need some gratification outside the relationship—whether from another person or another activity—that was not wanted before.

Even a couple with a good, working covenant may on occasion run into a particular problem that they cannot seem to solve by themselves. In such a case they would do well to consult a marital or couple therapist; an objective outside ear can often save a good deal of time and effort. Often only one or two sessions can clear up a troublesome matter.

The Graysons are a good example of a couple who worked out an excellent covenant and who have had a fine, rather traditional marriage for eighteen years.

Will, forty-seven, is eight years older than Jessica; they have a fifteen-year-old daughter and two sons, aged twelve and six.

For Will, marriage was out of the question until he knew he could support a wife and family. He became a skilled printer and has done moderately well over the years. Like Will, Jessica comes from a working-class background; she was an assembler in an electronics factory until she became pregnant. Since that time she has stayed at home.

The Graysons have always had a good relationship, but some years ago, when they were unable to agree about whether or not Will should give up his job and go into business, they had a few counseling sessions. A friend had offered Will a partnership in a printing firm and he was strongly attracted to the idea of being an independent businessman instead of an employee. But Jessica thought the venture too risky and she was opposed to their investing all their savings—plus borrowed money as well—in a business that might fail. Although Will seemed eager to go ahead, by the third visit to the therapist he realized that he, too, was anxious about the investment; he soon admitted that he was relieved that Jessica had kept him from making an impulsive move.

During that brief experience, the Graysons learned about covenants and set to work on their own. The process has worked extremely well for them ever since; they are an uncommonly harmonious couple. Because they communicate well and openly, and have deep love and respect for each other, they usually have little trouble resolving their differences. And neither of them ever thinks that those differences come up because one intends any harm or slight to the other.

The arguments they do have, now and then, are usually over money. Jessica feels that the "table allowance" Will gives her each week is adequate, but she resents having to ask for extra money when she needs it for clothes or something special. She is particularly annoyed when Will says they cannot afford an expenditure. At such times she is apt to suggest that Will does not earn as much as he could—and Will reminds her that he is very secure in his job, something they both wanted.

They try not to talk about these matters in front of the children. In fact, they usually wait until they are alone to discuss anything that is important or emotionally loaded. For the most part, they are openly affectionate to each other and to the children.

Their strong sense of family is evident in other ways, too. They do many things together, including camping vacations, and for the past few summers they have rented a lakeside cottage for a month. They often visit friends or other members of their families with the children. They also watch television together, and sometimes go to movies, the theater, or sports events. Will and the older boy like to watch some baseball and basketball games by themselves.

Will and Jessica go out by themselves in the evenings, too, and a couple of times a year they try to get away without the children for a weekend. They are not concerned about being away from the children on Sundays; they are not religious and do not go to church even though they were both raised as Methodists. They sent each child to Sunday School for a year and then let them decide whether or not to continue. They are truly laissez-faire about religion and have not been influenced or bothered by the criticism they receive periodically from their relatives and some of their friends.

Will feels that Jessica is not strict enough with the children—especially the fifteen-year-old daughter, who is very attractive and actively dating. But Jessica shrugs off the criticism and says Will wants her to be the disciplinarian because whenever that falls to him, he is even more easygoing than she is. None of the Graysons seems to be bothered by any of this and their family life is relaxed and pleasant.

Overall, the Graysons are family- and couple-oriented, although each spouse is a person and force. In spite of the fact that they are in quite traditional roles, Jessica is the more decisive tastemaker and pacesetter at home.

A summary of the covenant of this highly successful couple follows:

Category I.   Expectations of Marriage

They both see themselves as members of a family unit who are loving, loyal, and devoted to each other, as well as supports vis-à-vis the world—though they do not perceive the world as hostile. While they are aware of the current divorce rate, the Graysons are unthreatened by this and feel certain that they will stay together. They have never been bored with each other; Will explains, "I think we keep finding new things in one another. Like in sex, since we started reading and seeing more X-rated films we've learned to have a lot more fun."

They both take their responsibilities as parents seriously. Jessica feels that at times Will is not responsive enough to the children or to what she sees as emerging problems with the boys. Will worries too much about their daughter's potential for enjoying her attractiveness and sexuality. But when they are concerned as parents, Jessica and Will feel the children are a challenge as well as a joy to both of them and look to each other for companionship, comfort, and support.

Although money is frequently tight, they are not really upset about it because of Will's faith in his job. They manage to make ends meet by holding off on some extras so they can afford the essentials. For example, Will just spent several hundred dollars to repair their four-year-old car instead of buying a new one.

In sum, both feel that they are getting what they want and expect from their marriage. Neither has any unrealistic expectations of it or any hidden agenda.

Category II. Inner Needs

1. Independence-dependence

Although both feel quite independent, Will says he would be lost without Jessica: "Even though I know it's selfish, I've often thought that I hope to die first. (There's enough life insurance for her to live on.) I can't *imagine* living without Jess; I couldn't make it without her."

The Graysons generally go to the social events and movies that Jessica prefers, but that is fine with Will. He goes cheerfully, and even when the evening is disappointing, he is not resentful later because it was her choice.

When she is away (perhaps visiting her sick father in Florida), Will fares well. He is able to manage the household and younger children effectively for a week or so with his daughter's help.

Each of the Graysons is self-actualizing; they are reasonably independent and interdependent.

2. Activity-passivity

Basically, Will is less active than Jessica, although he is not a passive man and is respected among his fellow workers. Jessica initiates and follows through on most of the family activities—but they both regard this as her job.

They can both talk through their differences without continuing resentment.

3. Closeness-distance

Will seeks and needs more bodily intimacy than Jessica; he is a toucher. Jessica wants more emotional and verbal closeness, and this is difficult for Will; he tends to make jokes when emotions become too warm for him. Jessica regrets this; she misses the kind of intimacy she would like to have with him.

Fortunately, she has a circle of close women friends from whom she gets emotional support and understanding. Although they are not formally organized as a consciousness-raising group, they function as one.

Jessica's need for this kind of rapport and greater closeness troubles Will at times, but she accepts his difference in this area and neither resents it nor makes any effort to retaliate.

4. Power

Will uses the power of money almost as a manifestation of his masculine protest. He makes the money and is in charge of it. Much of this is theoretical, however, because Will is definitely a family man and most of the money is allocated and budgeted away before he brings home his check. Yet he does have the power to be arbitrary, and even though he rarely exercises that, it bothers Jessica. She plans to go back to work next year (when the youngest child will be seven and in school all day), and looks forward to her own income as the solution to this.

Jessica considered going to college—both Graysons, although blue-collar, are definitely of college-level intelligence—but decided to "leave college to the children." Although she did not tell Will why, she was afraid he would feel that she was "getting ahead of him." She reads a great deal and does not feel a consuming need for formal study.

5. Dominance-submission

There is good give and take; each accepts leadership from the other. Jessica has a slight edge, except for Will's use of money, but they complement each other well here.

6. Fear of Loneliness or Abandonment

Not a problem. Each is sure of the other.

7. Need to Possess and Control

These concepts do not apply to the Graysons, in spite of the fact that they are a traditional couple. They expect certain behavior from each other, and both of them give and receive it as a matter of course. Neither is defensively possessive or controlling of the other. They are secure; they *know* they are "right" for each other.

8. Level of and Response to Anxiety

Neither has a particular high level of anxiety. Jessica, however, is less well defended and so shows her anxiety more directly. She is not as sanguine about their financial security as her husband is.

Jessica is an attractive woman but she worries about her appearance and the first signs of aging. When she reveals this, Will responds with jokes or platitudinous reassurances, which she finds annoying. He, in turn, finds her annoyance manipulative—as if she expects him to give her more money for clothes, hairdressers, and so forth. To some extent, this leitmotif is accentuated for Jessica by the emergence of their daughter as an unusually attractive adolescent.

To a much greater extent than his wife, Will uses denial to deal with his anxiety. He plays safe and *feels* safe. The opposite of paranoid, he usually denies that he sees any dangers or threats to himself from others.

9. Gender Identity

Both Graysons feel good about themselves in their sex roles. Will feels that he has done well as a skilled worker and is now glad that he did not become an entrepreneur: "I get out of work at four and I don't have to think about it again until eight o'clock the next morning. I'm free!" The changing world has not threatened or touched Will very deeply. He is satisfied to move through life leaving bigger questions to others—although he is protective of his turf on those rare occasions when he actually recognizes a threat.

Jessica, on the other hand, is much more discontent and restless, as manifested by her anxiety about approaching middle age and her competition with her daughter. She does, however, feel sure of her desirability as a person and a woman, and Will reinforces her well— as she does him. Still, she has a growing concern about others seeing her as attractive. She does not want another man, but she *does* want reaffirmation of herself from Will.

10. Sexual Attraction to One Another

Objectively, each of the Graysons is an attractive person and they see each other that way. They have had a great resurgence of sexual activity over the past several years and they have no sexual dysfunctions: they are open and free in sex, have tried various positions, fellatio, cunnilingus, and they make frequent use of fantasy and of playing out their fantasies with one another. Although Jessica was sexually inhibited before their marriage, Will helped her to overcome this. She was a virgin and he was sexually experienced, but by the end of the first year of marriage Jessica was enjoying orgasms during coitus as well as during sex play.

JESSICA: "Sometimes just looking at him I get turned on again—that's how I got pregnant last time. After the youngest baby was born it took me a year to wholly enjoy sex again. That's when the porn books and movies were good for us. Maybe I'm a masochist. I like Will to be a little bit of a brute—I get turned on most when he really takes charge, and sometimes we play rape and I finally have to submit to him."

WILL: "I like to play the brute now and then. I also like being really passive—like she's my slave girl and knows just what to do to play with me and excite me—and she does!"

Although Jessica has been tempted a few times, she has never been sufficiently attracted to any man to risk upsetting her marriage. She believes it would not be worth it.

Will (unknown to Jessica) has had sex with other women four times—all when he was away from home and Jessica. He has never formed any relationship with another woman.

11. Acceptance (Love) of Self and Mate

The Graysons love themselves sufficiently to have good self-respect and they are truly in love with each other.

Passion between them has recently been rekindled to a high level.

12. Cognitive Style (and Approach to Problems)

The Graysons' cognitive styles, including intelligence, are similar.

Jessica is overly concerned with not challenging Will, wary that he might begin to doubt himself.

Exchanges

The major "in exchange-for" clause in the Graysons' covenant is that they will both stay in their traditional roles. Also, each says, in effect: "I will support you with love and sex, and reassure you about your masculinity/femininity."

Will supports Jessica's femininity in a teasing way, but for the most part she does not see this as hostile because she is well aware of her ability to excite him sexually.

The Graysons are basically satisfied with their life together. Although Jessica cannot get Will to be as open with her about his feelings as she would like, she accepts this without becoming unduly upset. They both feel that they have a good marriage compared to most of the other couples they know.

By and large their exchanges (quid pro quos) are designed to give them security with each other and within their slice of the world. They have fun, they argue, they disagree, they make good love, they play out their parental and Oedipal roles with their children, and life goes on with its ups and downs. The rises are not to great heights—but neither are the troughs very deep.

Category III.   Outside Problem Areas

1. Communication

Generally they send and receive messages clearly, except that Will withdraws when Jessica tries to discuss feelings and motivations that may underlie his behavior.

2. Lifestyle

Each has some of his/her own friends and several who are shared. Each has friends of the same gender. Their life centers on their family and friends.

3. Child Rearing

Each wants the other to be more strict with the children. Actually, the whole family has a warm, happy interaction most of the time.

4. Relationship with Children

Neither uses the children as allies against the other.

5. Family Myths

The family myth is that Will is where he is in life because he *wants* to be there, not because he *has* to. He believes—and Jessica goes along with the belief—that he could have become an entrepreneur but preferred to stay where he is and maintain his "proletarian" value system.

6. Values

Their values are similar. Will takes pride in Jessica's appearance and appreciates that he walks down the street with a woman other men look at. In return, she wants love and closeness—but she gets most of what she wants. She is proud to be with Will.

This summation of the Graysons' covenant was made possible because they did recently return for assistance from C.J.S. with a problem they could not work out themselves. Their covenant was reviewed in separate and joint sessions. These comments are from records of those sessions:

> I consider this couple an effective marital pair who are fulfilling their marital system's purposes as well as most of their individual needs. In essence, they have a single couple covenant. Their individual covenants are congruent and complementary, with minimum conflict. Communication is reasonably good. Above all, they recognize their importance to each other and both are willing to put themselves out to make the relationship work. They genuinely love one another. Recognizing that their sexual and gender reinforcement needs were a source of potential trouble if they did not find sufficient gratification with each other, they turned to a new sexual freedom within their marriage—and thereby enhanced their lives.
>
> The Graysons appear as two adult partners, each of whom has a childlike secondary theme. They are able to switch roles and to be unconsciously sensitive when the other is childlike and needs support, although Will is not quite as adept at giving support as is Jessica. At the time they married, Will was probably more of a parental partner for Jessica than he is today.
>
> Their defenses are generally used in a positive way, eliciting only minimal negative reactions in the partner. Jessica has learned to respect Will's need for emotional distance and not to be bothered by his modest masculine protest. He is often bemused and makes

light of Jessica's anxiety about her attractiveness, while giving her the basic reassurance she asks for. They respect each other, including each other's defenses and foibles.

And so, you might well be asking, what could possibly bring this couple to a therapist's office? The problem that cropped up was, oddly, an outgrowth of their renewed sexual passion.

After the last child was born, the Graysons agreed that they did not want any more children. Up until this time they had relied on a diaphragm for contraception, and while Jessica always found it a bother—and frequently disruptive—she was willing to go along with it because she could risk not using it now and then when the situation warranted it; they had always wanted three children and an accidental pregnancy would not have been a catastrophe. Now, however, the family was complete and Jessica switched to the pill.

All went well for six years. Then, for medical reasons, Jessica's gynecologist told her that she would have to change to some other method of birth control and advised her to go back to the diaphragm. Jessica resisted, asked about an IUD instead. The doctor explained that while it was a possibility, he felt it might bring on complications and did not like to recommend it. This cooled Jessica's interest in the device.

But now she had a dilemma. She and Will had never felt so free and joyous about sex before; more than ever, she felt that the interruption of inserting a diaphragm would spoil their pleasure, even change their lives. She asked Will to have a vasectomy.

It had never occurred to her that he might refuse. She knew he disliked condoms as much as she did, and coitus interruptus was certainly out of the question—so that had always left contraception up to her. She had accepted the responsibility all these years and now she felt that it was time for him to assume it. She was sure he would agree—but he did not. Together, they carefully researched vasectomy and learned all the facts. They were familiar with the procedure, and knew that with the newest techniques the likelihood of the operation's being reversible was better than it had been in the past, but repair was far from 100 percent sure. Although Will knew intellectually that the vasectomy would not diminish his masculinity, sexual desire, ability, or pleasure, he still felt that it would make him "less of a man" because his ejaculate would not be fertile.

The Graysons simply could not work this one out. Nothing Will could think of to offer as a trade was important enough to make Jessica feel that he was being reasonable. To the Graysons' credit, they were able to discuss the question at length while maintaining great respect and feeling for each other. Neither was angry with the other. Jessica was honestly looking for a means of contraception that would not interfere with their spontaneity; Will understood and agreed with all her feelings—but he knew that he could not live with a vasectomy. They were at an impasse.

They found the solution to the problem in two therapy sessions. Jessica explained the predicament and said, "Since it would be so simple for Will to have a vasectomy, isn't it wrong for him to refuse?" My reply was that there was no right or wrong to it. Will felt as he did, after knowing all the facts, and it would therefore be unwise for him to have the operation even if he were to agree to it. Jessica could see that this was so. I added that I, as a male, could empathize with Will's feelings—and then suggested that instead of interrupting their lovemaking, Jessica might insert the diaphragm every night just as routinely as she brushed her teeth. Simple as this idea was, apparently they had never thought of it.

The unbiased confirmation of a third person reassured Jessica that Will's reluctance was not selfish or even within his control; she agreed to see how the new system worked out for a time. It is too soon to know what will happen, and if she continues to feel discontent they may have to return for further exploration.

Even if they do, this is a comparatively minor problem for the Graysons. They will encounter a much larger one next year when Jessica goes back to work. At that time, the entire structure of their marriage will change and their covenant may need major revisions.

Given the covenant they have, the extent of their experience, and the quality of their love, the chances are excellent that Will and Jessica will be able to make the necessary adjustments themselves. And if they run into any trouble, they know where they can get help.

They know, too, that nothing that happens to them is likely to divide them in any serious sense. They are not two people with two covenants, each discontent because their expectations and needs can never be met. Instead, they work together, united by their understanding of what each wants from and will give to the other. They will have some disagreements and some disappointments, just as they have had in the past. But they will always know *why* they disagree, what it is that each of them wants, and the reason the other cannot go along with it. They will respect each other's needs because they understand them. They will never say to each other—as so many couples do—"I don't know what it is you want" or worse, "I don't know what *I* want."

This is the essence of a couple covenant. It is a key tool that can help you and your mate, like the Graysons, to know yourselves and each other, and to work, within the framework of that knowledge, to fulfill each of your needs, and your needs and responsibilities as a couple.

No matter how much or how little you consciously use the covenant principle, you will almost certainly find that it helps you make a lot more sense of what goes on between you and your mate. Your covenants do exist, whether you make the effort to clarify them or not.

If you choose to *work* on your covenant, you and your partner are likely to go far in developing the best relationship you can possibly have: a relationship characterized by openness, sharing, support, trust, and intimacy—in short, the highest order of love.

Appendix

A Guide to Writing Your Private Covenant

As you have seen, different people use different styles in setting forth their covenants. You can use any style that is comfortable and natural for you.

For a preliminary appraisal of your relationship, see the following form:*

1. What are your expectations from your marriage/couple relationship?

2. Which of your expectations do you feel are being met?

3. Which of your expectations do you feel are *not* being met?

4. What personality traits or behavior of your partner would you like to see changed?

5. What do you feel you would like to change about yourself?

6. Are there any private hopes or plans you have been reluctant to share with your partner, even though you have wanted to? If so, what are they?

7. How do the two of you make decisions or resolve fights?

8. Is there anything else you would like to add about your relationship?

---

* The authors are indebted to Ilona Sena, M.S.W., who developed these questions for use in short-term couple therapy at the Jewish Board of Family and Children's Services in New York City.

PRIVATE COVENANT WORKSHEET

Category (start each one on new page)		Level of Awareness (Check One)		
I. My Expectations of the Relationship; **II.** Expectations that Arise from My Inner Needs; **III.** Apparently External Problem Areas.				
		Verbalized	*Conscious but not Verbalized*	*Unconscious (Beyond Awareness)*
Number	***Statement:*** Include what you want and what you will give in exchange; what problems these items cause.			

This simple form will make you think and get you started. When you are ready to write out your covenant, make yourself a worksheet like this one (using as many pages as you need).

REMINDERS

Here is a reminder list that will serve as a quick review of the principles of the covenant. For more detail, turn back to Chapter 4.

CAUTION: Don't be surprised (or upset) if your covenant is inconsistent because you have strong contradictory wants or needs. For example, you may want to be independent and at the same time need to have your partner approve of whatever you do. This is not abnormal; every covenant contains some contradictions.

Each covenant has three levels of awareness:

Conscious and verbalized

These are items you have been in the habit of discussing with each other, although they are not always heard by the listener.

Conscious but not verbalized

These are parts of your covenant that you are aware of but do not share with your partner because you fear his/her anger or disapproval, or because you feel embarrassed or shy.

Beyond awareness

These are aspects of your covenant that are beyond your usual awareness. You may have an idea of what some of them are. They are often felt as "warning lights" in your head, fleeting feelings of concern· that get pushed away. Do the best you can with these.

Remember that each of you acts as if the other knew the terms of his/her covenant. Although you never actually agreed on them, you both feel angered, hurt, or betrayed when you think that the other does not fulfill his/her part of your covenant. In each area, note where you think your mate has failed in his or her part of the bargain. Do not worry about being fair. Write down what you *really feel* about this behavior.

Covenant terms—wants, expectations, and what you are willing to give in exchange, as well—fall into three general categories. This reminder list consists of those three categories. Under each heading there is a list of areas that are common sources of trouble. You have probably thought of some of them yourself but may have overlooked others.

This guide is offered to help you write out or talk through your own private covenant. If you do the former, do not show it to your partner until you have started to work together—and then reveal only as much as you feel comfortable in doing at any one session:

1. Make worksheets and use them. Start each category on a new page.

2. Respond to all items that are meaningful to you; skip the others.

3. Include all areas in which you feel your partner has not stuck to the bargain. Be specific. State how you feel about it.

4. Answer in terms of today. If something from the past still bothers you, say so.

5. Make your answers as long or as short as you like, but do not merely answer "Yes" or "No." To be useful, your answers must convey your feelings. The effort to articulate your feelings in writing may actually help you understand them better.

6. For your own convenience, since you may want to refer back some time, write clearly or type. You might use Roman numerals for the categories and item numbers that conform to the lists which follow, such as II:3; III:5.

7. Do not try to work on more than one category at a sitting. Note that these lists are only *reminders* of possibilities that we suggest you consider. Add any other items that are meaningful to you.

REMINDER LIST
(SEE CHAPTER 4 FOR FULLER EXPLANATIONS)

Category I   My Expectations of the Relationship

I expect—or I don't expect:

1. A loyal, devoted, loving, and exclusive mate.
2. A constant support vis-à-vis the rest of the world.
3. Insurance against loneliness.
4. To be part of a couple.
5. A panacea for life's stresses.
6. A relationship that will last "until death do us part."
7. Sanctioned and readily available sex.
8. To create a family.
9. The inclusion in my new family of children, parents, friends, etc.

10. To acquire a family, not just a mate.

11. To have my own home-refuge away from the world.

12. To have a respectable position and status in society.

13. The creation of an economic/social unit.

14. To be an image that will inspire us both to work, build, accumulate.

15. A respectable cover for aggressive drives.

Make sure you have included any areas in which you feel that your mate has let you down. Say how you feel about it.

Write out a summary of what you want from your relationship in Category I and *what you will give in excharge for it.*

Category II   Expectations that Arise from My Inner Needs

These are the items that come from psychological and biological needs. They are often beyond awareness—but still, you do have some ideas about them.

1. Am I independent or dependent?

2. Am I active or passive?

3. Do I want closeness and intimacy, or do I prefer distance?

4. Who has more power? How do I feel about it?

5. Who submits, who dominates? Is there an equal give and take of leadership?

6. Do I fear abandonment and loneliness?

7. Do I try to possess and control?

8. What triggers anxiety in me? How do I cope with it? How do I cope with my mate's anxiety?

9. How do I feel about myself as a man or a woman?

10. What physical and personality characteristics are important to me in a mate? How does he/she measure up? If poorly, what is missing? Do I like his/her attitudes about sex? Are they like mine? Do we have sex-related problems?

11. Can I love myself and my mate?

12. How do we approach problems? Are our styles the same or different? Do we accept and appreciate the differences or do they cause trouble?

Add anything else that you think is a problem area. Be specific.

Write out a summary of what you want from your relationship in Category II and *what you will give in exchange for it.*

Category III   Apparently External Problem Areas

1. Communication.
2. Intellectual differences.
3. Energy level.
4. Interests.
5. Original families.
6. Child rearing.
7. Alliances with children.
8. Family myths.
9. Money.
10. Scx.
11. Values.
12. Friends.
13. Gender- and interest-determined roles and responsibilities.

Add any items not mentioned here that are significant.

How do you usually react when you feel that you have been let down or deceived? How does your partner react?

Write out a summary of what you want from your relationship in Category III and *what you will give in exchange for it.*

Catalog

If you are interested in a list of fine Paperback books, covering a wide range of subjects and interests, send your name and address, requesting your free catalog, to:

McGraw-Hill Paperbacks
1221 Avenue of Americas
New York, N.Y. 10020